The Generals' Tea Party

Previously Published

The Empire Builders

The Generals' Tea Party

by Boris Vian

Translated by
Simon Watson Taylor

Grove Press, Inc.
New York

Le Goûter des généraux was first produced at the Théâtre Gaîté-Montparnasse, Paris, on September 24, 1965, directed by François Maistre and designed by François Robert.

The Generals' Tea Party, translated from the French by Simon Watson Taylor, was first produced in London at the Jeanetta Cochrane Theatre by the London Traverse Theatre Company on November 8, 1966, with the following cast:

General JAMES AUDUBON WILSON DE LA PETARDIERE-FRENOUILLOU	*Richard Murdoch*
Madame DE LA PETARDIERE	*Gwen Nelson*
ROBERT	*Duncan Livingstone*
LEON PLANTIN	*Antony Kenway*
General DUPONT-D'ISIGNY	*Russell Hunter*
General LENVERS DE LAVESTE	*Richardson Morgan*
General JUILLET	*Richard Mayes*
Monseigneur ROLAND TAPECUL	*Richard Beale*
FRANCINE	*Virginia Wetherell*
General KORKILOFF	*Gwen Nelson*
General JACKSON	*Richard Beale*
General CHING PING TING	*Roy Hanlon*

Directed by Michael Geliot, designed by Ralph Koltai, music by Guy Wolfenden, played by E. D. Riches as trumpeter.

Photographs from the London production by John Haynes.

Characters

General JAMES AUDUBON WILSON DE LA PETARDIERE-
    FRENOUILLOU
Madame DE LA PETARDIERE, *mother of the General*
ROBERT, *Audubon's orderly and manservant*
LEON PLANTIN, *Prime Minister*
General DUPONT-D'ISIGNY ⎫
General LENVERS DE LAVESTE ⎬ *Audubon's* G.H.Q.
General JUILLET ⎭
Monseigneur ROLAND TAPECUL, *Archbishop of Paris*
FRANCINE, *Plantin's secretary*
General KORKILOFF, *Military Delegate of the U.S.S.R.*
General JACKSON, *Military Delegate of the U.S.A.*
General CHING PING TING, *Military Delegate of China*

Act One: The Paris home of General Audubon
Act Two: The offices of the Prime Minister
Act Three: An underground command post

Translator's Note on the Text

Two typescripts of the text of this play exist, one of an earlier and largely different version, the other a revised text which was that published by Ed. Jean-Jacques Pauvert in the volume *Théâtre* and first produced in Paris at the Gaîté-Montparnasse in September, 1965. This translation is based on the revised text, but incorporates a number of marginal additions and revisions inserted by the author in a copy of the earlier typescript which were certainly intended to be transferred to the "definitive" version. These additions and revisions are not included in the Pauvert edition of the play, but can be found as footnotes in the original published edition, that by the Collège de 'Pataphysique in their *Dossier 18-19* (1962).

This English version may be considered a "free translation" insofar as it takes occasional liberties with the French text—liberties dictated by the fact that the play is full of recondite jokes and allusions and untranslatable puns. The private jokes had to be made more accessible to the English-speaking reader (and playgoer) at the cost, sometimes, of padding the text, and the puns had to be remolded, where possible, or comparable substitutes invented. Let one single example suffice as an illustration of both these problems: at the end of the last act General Korkiloff is initiating his colleagues into the mysteries of Russian Roulette. Holding the revolver and twirling the cylinder, the Russian general explains: *"Vous laissez une cartouche dedans . . . vous faites tourner barillet . . . comme loterie . . ."* and is interrupted by General Laveste with the mysterious query: *"Et Grédy?"* Explanation: *"barillet"* = cylinder of revolver, but also happens to be the surname of a successful French writer of boulevard comedies, in collaboration with a M. Grédy. I hope that my substitution of "You leave one bullet in gun . . . then make cylinder spin, so . . . like in bingo. . . ," "Bingo bango bongo, I don't want to leave the Congo . . ." is neither more nor less gratuitous than the original.

S. W. T.

Act One
Scene One

A room in the home of General James Audubon Wilson de la Pétardière-Frenouillou. Pretentious and old-fashioned bourgeois furniture, redolent of the presence of an aging mother with fetid breath. When the curtain goes up, one can see on the right the open door of a bathroom and hear through it the sound of General AUDUBON *singing as he performs his ablutions. A few moments later he appears on stage, a rather weakly looking individual, fifty-five or so, nervous—or rather petulant—in manner. He is in shirt-sleeves, collarless, his trousers supported by suspenders. After rubbing his face dry, he lays the towel over the back of a chair. Still humming, he goes up to the mirror and makes a great effort to attach his collar to his shirt and infiltrate his tie into the collar. He makes five or six increasingly fumbling efforts to achieve this, and remains unsuccessful. Finally, he yelps with rage, then in a terrible tantrum stamps his feet on the ground, and calls out in exasperation.*

AUDUBON: Oh, drat it! Mama! Mama! Oh, I'm absolutely furious! *Mama!*

MOTHER (*voice off-stage*): What is it *now,* you naughty boy? (*She appears: she is a repulsive creature, dignified, white-haired.*) What *is* the matter?

AUDUBON: Oh! It's so exasperating. It's this tie. I just can't get the knot tied.

MOTHER: Come now, Audubon, don't get excited. You only have to ask your mama.

9

AUDUBON: Oh! I just can't bear things resisting me like that! It's so humiliating!

MOTHER: No, no, Audubon, there's nothing humiliating about it. This is mere manual work, whereas *you* were created to think, to reflect, not to use your hands like any clodhopper.

AUDUBON: But I'm a general, mother . . .

MOTHER: Yes, indeed, and the brain of your body of troops.

AUDUBON: Not "body," mama, "corps." In my case, "army corps." A full general commands an army corps, a brigadier general commands a brigade, and a lieutenant general commands a division.

MOTHER (*knotting his tie*): Ah well, Audubon, as your late father always told you, in your army corps you must be the brain which commands and which is always obeyed smoothly by the organization's innumerable cogwheels, by virtue of the soothing and mollifying oil which constitutes discipline. There, look how nicely I've tied your tie.

AUDUBON (*kisses her hand*): Mother, you're an absolute darling.

MOTHER: Ah, Audubon, if it wasn't for me you'd fly into a tantrum twenty times a day. Now, have you washed your feet well?

AUDUBON: Yes, of course I have, mother.

MOTHER: And your ears, too?

He nods "yes."

Well, I'm going to have a look, Audubon, to make sure. I remember very well what a struggle it was trying to clean your ears when you were six years old. (*She inspects them.*) Hmm. This ear looks a bit dubious, my boy.

AUDUBON: Oh, you can't have looked properly, mama. I'll show you. (*He picks up the towel and proffers it to her by one corner. She studies it, nods her head and puts it back.*)

MOTHER: That's a good boy. Ah, Audubon, how sweet your little ears were when you were tiny. But here you are now—a great big grown-up military booby getting into even worse scrapes than when you were a little boy and dipped the kitten into the soup to give her extra energy.

She laughs. He sulks.

AUDUBON: Mother, must you always bring up these old stories?

MOTHER: All right, Audubon, I know that young people don't like being reminded of their childhood. But we are alone, so there's no reason for you to be shy. For me, you will always be the little boy who could never tie his shoelaces by himself.

AUDUBON: I can tie them all by myself now, mother.

MOTHER: But who has to tie your tie!

A bell rings.

Well, I wonder who that can be? Were you expecting a visitor?

AUDUBON: Why, no, mother.

MOTHER (*shaking her finger at him*): Audubon, Audubon,

I know you, you little rogue, that's another skirt at the door, isn't it?

AUDUBON: Oh, mama! How could you even think such a thing? (*But he giggles, feeling rather flattered.*) Robert!

(*He calls louder.*) Robert! Will you go to the door.

ROBERT (*voice off-stage*): All right, all right.

Sound of footsteps—voice saying "Yes, sir," and the noise of a door opened and closed again.

MOTHER: I'll leave you alone, my son. (*She leaves the room.*)

Enter LEON PLANTIN, *followed by* ROBERT.

ROBERT: It's the Prime Minister, sir. (*He springs to attention.*)

AUDUBON: Very well, dismiss. (*To* PLANTIN:) My dear Prime Minister . . .

ROBERT *leaves the room.*

PLANTIN: Good old Audubon.

They embrace each other affectionately.

AUDUBON: What a splendid surprise!

PLANTIN: Not for me . . .

AUDUBON: What do you mean, not for you? (*Aside.*) Damn rude, this fellow.

PLANTIN: I mean it's not a surprise for me because I knew I was coming to see you.

AUDUBON: Ah, yes, of course. Please sit down, my dear Prime Minister. Won't you have something to drink? A lemon barley-water perhaps?

PLANTIN: Hmm . . . Don't you have any Pernod?

AUDUBON: Ah . . . no, only anisette . . . but surely even that's a bit strong at this hour of day?

PLANTIN: I'd have preferred Pernod, really—oh well, let's have a look at your anisette. Tell me, Wilson, can you face facts?

AUDUBON: If you mean the enemy . . . (*he draws himself up proudly*) . . . a Wilson de la Pétardière is always ready to face . . .

PLANTIN: No, no, no, for goodness sake, the situation isn't that grave. (*Sigh.*) Not yet.

AUDUBON: Oh, good, good. That makes me feel better. (*He starts fussing around.*) Now let me get you your anisette.

PLANTIN: Very little water, please.

AUDUBON *hands him a glass, he drinks.*

Ugh! How disgusting! This isn't anisette, man!

AUDUBON: Oh dear! Please excuse me . . . I must have given you my barley-water by mistake. How careless of me. (*He exchanges glasses, then sits down.*)

PLANTIN: I'd have preferred a Pernod, but still . . . (*He drinks and shudders.*) Ugh! It's not much better than your barley-water. (*He puts down his glass.*) I don't think I'm really thirsty after all. (*He looks around him.*) Why, what a nice place you've got here.

AUDUBON (*modestly*): Oh . . . it's very simple, really. This is my bachelor-study, where I entertain my friends . . . we are so much more comfortable here. (*Gives a wink*.) This is my mother's apartment really, but she's so broad-minded . . . Every week she lets me give a little party here for a few friends.

PLANTIN (*sarcastic*): My goodness, what fun! Are there any women at these little parties?

AUDUBON: But of course. Well, sometimes. Some married men bring their wives and the others often bring their mothers. It's really very gay.

PLANTIN (*disappointed*): Oh yes, charming! Well, my dear Wilson, I'm going to get straight down to brass tacks with you: the present situation in Europe is very grave.

AUDUBON (*solemn expression*): Ah . . .

PLANTIN (*forcefully*): Yes. At this very moment we are faced with a concatenation of absolutely unpredictable and completely unforeseen events. I take it that you follow the economic situation closely?

AUDUBON (*solemnly*): Gracious me, with great interest, of course, like all those of us upon whom destiny has thrust the mantle of responsibility.

PLANTIN: I admire your resolute spirit. Let me come to the point.

AUDUBON: Please do.

PLANTIN: Have you seen what the cows are doing?

AUDUBON: The cows?

PLANTIN: And the hens?

AUDUBON: What do you mean, the hens?

PLANTIN: And the miners?

AUDUBON: Euh . . . what about the miners?

PLANTIN: My dear Wilson, the cows are calfing, the hens are laying, and the miners are digging coal.

AUDUBON: But . . . euh . . . is that so serious?

PLANTIN: Well, under normal circumstances, you see, there's nothing serious about it because we simply bring the law of supply and demand into play, you see . . .

AUDUBON (*who doesn't see at all but pretends he does*): Ah yes, the law . . . of course. We bring it into play . . . like this . . . (*imitating a see-saw*).

PLANTIN: No, not at all . . . like this (*imitating an accordion*). However, apart from the fact that at the present moment such an operation is impossible, we are confronted with the particularly annoying fact that all these circumstances are concomitant. We must pull out all stops to economic harmony, no soft-pedaling.

AUDUBON (*bewildered*): I must confess . . . euh . . . that I'm not too well briefed in these questions. . . . Could you perhaps explain in greater detail? You know, I'm only . . . ah, hmm . . . a simple soldier . . . rough and ready . . . rather coarse . . . at home in practical matters . . .

PLANTIN: That's true, forgive me. (*Supercilious laugh.*) I do tend to get carried away by the vocabulary of my previous profession . . .

AUDUBON: Of *course*, you used to be . . . euh . . .?

PLANTIN: Chief organist at the Sacré-Coeur. Anyhow, to sum up the situation briefly, we are suffering at present from a crisis of overproduction. In ordinary times, when the gross agricultural product *increases,* we arrange for the gross industrial product to *decrease*; as a result, agricultural prices drop and industrial prices rise; at this point, we grant a subsidy to the farmers who are thus able to restore and maintain their previous price levels, while at the same time we raise the wages of the industrial workers so as to allow them to take advantage of the abundance of agricultural produce available; the subsidy granted to the farmers is used by them to buy industrial equipment; the industrialists consequently realize enormous profits; and we pocket those profits by imposing compulsory contributions to public funds, taxes on productivity, purchase taxes, capital gains taxes, and various penalties and fines inflicted by the ministry's inspectorate. The circle is closed and everybody's happy.

AUDUBON (*who still hasn't understood a word, stubbornly*): But in the end we soldiers always get a raw deal.

PLANTIN: No, no, not at all, Wilson, you do just as well as the other branches of the bureaucracy. Don't be bitter now. I have just explained to you a method of balancing the budget which all parties have been using for years, and I don't remember having heard the military complain about the credits they are voted.

AUDUBON: Well, perhaps. But I still don't see why the present situation is so serious.

PLANTIN: But, Audubon, it's frightening. At present, agricultural production is increasing *at the same time* as industrial production. As you can well imagine, it is impossible to achieve any balance under such conditions.

AUDUBON: Couldn't we shoot a few of the ringleaders?

PLANTIN: No, no, Audubon, that would be only a temporary palliative. We must canalize all this productivity, find new outlets for it.

AUDUBON: The consumers, perhaps?

PLANTIN: The consumers, yes, but it's dangerous to let them get used to abundance. Dangerous and unhealthy. Abundance is emollient, Audubon. Austerity is the very lifeblood of a healthy state. But you're getting warm. Go on, try again. Now, what is the ideal consumer?

AUDUBON (*thinks, then his face lights up as he exclaims*): The army!

PLANTIN: Right! The army presents this essential advantage, Audubon: it is the consumer who pays the army, and it is the army which consumes. Whence a permanent imbalance which alone allows us to achieve balance. Because, as any dunce can understand, it's impossible to achieve a balance unless there's an imbalance to start with.

AUDUBON (*admiringly*): You know, we men of the sword do tend to underrate the intelligence of you men of State . . . But what you have just told me is really . . . very powerful.

PLANTIN (*flattered*): You are too kind.

AUDUBON: No, no, I mean it. Very powerful indeed. A little anisette?

PLANTIN: That, on the contrary, is not very powerful . . .

however, since you don't have any Pernod . . . (*He holds out his glass.*)

AUDUBON (*breaks off suddenly*): But, listen, Léon! You're not suggesting . . . !

PLANTIN: Yes. War.

AUDUBON: War! (*He puts his glass on the table with a shaking hand, then collapses into an armchair.*)

PLANTIN: Come, come, pull yourself together, my dear fellow . . . Wilson! . . . well, really.

AUDUBON: Ah . . . Léon . . . It's not possible . . . Aaah . . . quick . . . give me my barley-water . . . there . . . over there . . .

PLANTIN *goes to the table, picks up the glass of anisette by mistake and hands it to him.* AUDUBON *swallows it in one gulp and smacks his lips.*

Ah! . . . that's better.

PLANTIN (*taking the other glass*): Come! Here's to your health, my dear fellow! (*He drinks.*) Ugh! How disgusting! This is your confounded barley-water again. And you've drunk my anisette. (*Takes Audubon's glass.*)

AUDUBON: That's too bad . . . to hell with avarice. What a shock you gave me. War, indeed! Don't make jokes like that, please!

PLANTIN: Listen, Wilson, this is no joke.

AUDUBON (*vaguely*): Ah, I'm dreaming! Marvelous feeling!

PLANTIN (*coldly*): My dear friend, you are not very funny.

AUDUBON (*coming to himself again*): Ha, nor are you!

PLANTIN: The leaders of industry and agriculture are counting on you. You must look facts in the face and accept your responsibilities.

AUDUBON: Well, I don't know about that. A general isn't responsible for starting wars. It is always civilians who declare them.

PLANTIN: What are you afraid of? You will have five million businessmen behind you.

AUDUBON: Yes, but what will I have in front of me? A lot of characters brandishing rifles and sabers and pointing guns at me. Do you think that's funny?

PLANTIN: But look here, it's your job to make war, goddamn it.

AUDUBON: It's my job to be a general, and believe me it's not much fun under these conditions. Oh, it's a great job in peacetime; regular promotion, plenty of leisure, and there's no risk of seeing young men promoted over your head just because they've done a bit of fighting! —It's only the amateurs who are silly enough to get themselves involved in fighting, they don't see the danger involved! But in wartime, with our total strength going up and down all the time, and the noise and the confusion . . . Oh, it's a thankless job, I can tell you.

PLANTIN: But the entire country will be behind you!

AUDUBON: Just now it was the businessmen, now it's the whole country. What about your last election? Seventy-five per cent abstained from voting.

PLANTIN: That's another argument in our favor! Silence means approval!

AUDUBON: Do you know what I think? I think you're batty.

PLANTIN: Pass the anisette.

AUDUBON: There's none left.

PLANTIN: Then send your orderly down to buy a bottle of Pernod.

> AUDUBON *is about to protest.*

Go on. I'll pay.

> AUDUBON *calls.*

AUDUBON: Robert!

> *Enter* ROBERT.

ROBERT: Yes, General de la Pétardière, sir.

PLANTIN: Here's five hundred of the folding stuff, Robert, go out and buy us a bottle of Pernod.

ROBERT: That costs eight hundred, Mr. Prime Minister, sir.

PLANTIN: Goodness, how stingy can you get! When I think of the money we squander on the armed forces. (*He hands over a thousand francs and takes the five hundred back.*) That's a thousand francs, bring me back the change.

ROBERT: Yes, sir. (*Exit.*)

PLANTIN: Hmm . . . Where were we?

AUDUBON: I had just told you you were batty, and to prove how right I was, you asked me for more anisette although you said a short while before that you couldn't stand it.

PLANTIN: Ugh! Your revolting anisette!

AUDUBON: Never mind about that. I still think you're out of your mind. In any case, nobody enjoys war unless there's something wrong with his sex life—it's in the Kinsey Report.

PLANTIN: Or peace, either, especially if he's a general.

AUDUBON (*in desperation*): But it's very dangerous, don't you realize? During the last war, some generals were even killed.

PLANTIN: They were German generals.

AUDUBON: But we're allies of the Germans now. And then there were generals taken prisoner. Giraud for instance, an absolutely unheard of thing to happen! And Darlan was killed, and a lot of perfectly dreadful things like that happened. It's no joke any longer, being a general. One really has to risk one's skin these days.

PLANTIN: Come now, some of them have done very nicely for themselves. Memoirs and all that. In any case, it is essential for you to give me your agreement today.

AUDUBON: Well, let me tell you that there's only one thing that's essential when it comes to protecting the life of a soldier, I mean a career soldier of course, and that is prudence. Look at 1914. Now there was a sensible war. All those trenches. We had plenty of time to spare in the trenches, and we could see what we were doing. And then as well as a front there was a rear filled with pretty little female allies. . . . Ah yes, the fourteen-eighteen war will never be improved upon.

PLANTIN: What were you in the Great War?

AUDUBON: I was A.D.C. to the G.I.C. at G.H.Q. Ah, what happy memories those times bring back to me. The Somme in springtime. Verdant Verdun.

PLANTIN: God help the army of today. I come here to offer you a brand-new modern war and all you can do is to bleat about the one before bloody last.

AUDUBON: I know of no general who has ever encouraged his country to go to war.

PLANTIN: What about Bonaparte?

AUDUBON: Bonaparte? Oh, he was a nasty coarse little Corsican corporal! He couldn't care less if the French fought a war! You're not going to tell me that it was a Corsican army which invaded Russia in 1812, are you?

PLANTIN: You're talking a lot of damn nonsense.

AUDUBON: I don't care. In any case, in these days when everybody is so intellectual and profound, talking nonsense is the only way of proving that one has a free and independent mentality.

PLANTIN (*rising*): Well, I'm wasting my time arguing with you, really: the bill has already been voted. I wanted to appeal to your common sense, but since that seems a hopeless task you can consider it an order.

AUDUBON: An order?

PLANTIN: Yes. From the Nation.

AUDUBON (*realizing delightedly*): But under those circumstances it's quite different. You'll cover up for me?

PLANTIN: Of course.

AUDUBON (*unhesitatingly*): Right then, I agree. For when?

PLANTIN: As soon as possible.

AUDUBON (*eagerly*): Certainly. You can count on me.

ROBERT *enters.*

Ah, there you are! Uncork the bottle, you big oaf. We're going to drink a toast. Come on, get on with it.

PLANTIN: So from now on you'll take charge of everything?

AUDUBON: Will you go on covering up for me?

PLANTIN: Naturally.

AUDUBON (*self-confidently*): Then I'll take charge of every-thing.

ROBERT: Here's the Pernod, General de la Pétardière, sir!

AUDUBON: Let us raise our glasses.

He and PLANTIN *clink glasses.*

Drink with us, soldier!

ROBERT *pours himself a drink.*

To Victories! *La gloire!*

He takes a swig of his drink and chokes violently. PLANTIN *and* ROBERT *pound him on the back.*

PLANTIN: Take it easy!

AUDUBON: That stuff really is powerful! Quite different from anisette. (*He holds out his glass.*) Fill it up, Robert. (*He swigs the second glassful like an old hand.*)

PLANTIN: Well, you're learning fast! (*Aside.*) And he drinks it neat! (*To* ROBERT:) Give him another one.

AUDUBON: Ahhh . . . that's good. (*To* ROBERT:) What are you fiddling around with there?

ROBERT: I've brought you back the change, sir.

AUDUBON: You may keep it.

ROBERT: Right, thank you, sir.

PLANTIN: Hey, look here, you . . .

AUDUBON: Oh, don't be mean! This is war, isn't it!

PLANTIN (*grumbling*): And this is one that's costing me a bundle!

AUDUBON: Now, if you please, I'll ask you to retire so that I can set to work.

PLANTIN: Are you going to have a conference with your colleagues?

AUDUBON: Right away. A camp conference.

PLANTIN: That's the spirit! (*He rises.*) Robert, my hat.

ROBERT: Yes, Mr. Prime Minister, sir. (*Goes off to look for Plantin's hat and coat and returns with them.*) If the Prime Minister would deign to assume his garments.

While ROBERT *is holding out the coat for* PLANTIN *to put on,* AUDUBON *is standing in the background practicing a Napoleonic pose.*

PLANTIN: Robert! (*In a low voice.*) Give me back that two hundred. I haven't a sou for my taxi. (*He gestures to him to give back the change.*)

ROBERT (*in a loud voice*): What did you say, sir?

AUDUBON *jerks out of his private reverie and comes up to them.*

PLANTIN: Nothing! Nothing! Good-by.

AUDUBON: Good-by.

ROBERT: This way, sir.

AUDUBON (*alone*): War! What a bore that fellow **Plantin** is! As if I didn't have anything better to do! (*He goes up to the low table on which the bottle is standing surrounded by discarded glasses, then, looking around him in a thoroughly guilty manner, quickly pours himself out a drink and gulps it down.*) Hmm. Not bad at all. (*He inspects the bottle's label.*) With water added, it's almost the same color as barley-water. (*He takes the bottle and goes to put it away in his cupboard, then comes back. He picks up a glass, hesitates, goes over and pours himself another shot, swallows it, and comes back once again.*) Mama! Oh, mother dear!

MOTHER (*voice off-stage*): Are you calling me?

Enter MME. DE LA PETARDIERE.

AUDUBON: Mama, I'd like to ask you a favor . . .

MOTHER: By all means, dear boy. I should be only too delighted to grant you anything within reason.

AUDUBON: Mama, I'd like to invite a few little chums of mine around this afternoon. May I?

MOTHER: Are they well-brought-up boys?

AUDUBON: Oh yes, mother, *very* well brought up. They are all generals. My G.H.Q.

MOTHER: If they are nice boys, Audubon, I see no reason to refuse you. Invite your little chums along for a tea party.

AUDUBON: Mama, could you perhaps bake us a sponge cake?

MOTHER (*indulgently*): Ah, I can see what you're up to. You're taking advantage of my soft-heartedness.

AUDUBON: Oh! You are sweet, mama.

MOTHER: But tell me, what's the reason for this celebration?

AUDUBON: Oh, nothing, just to have a gossip, to see each other again . . . they are all old friends of mine.

MOTHER: You're hiding something from me, Audubon. (*She sniffs.*) Come here.

He goes up to her.

Breathe out.

He blows out a very quick breath.

Harder.

He goes "ha" in her face.

Oh! How disgusting. (*She gives him a resounding slap.*)

You've been drinking. You stink of absinthe.

AUDUBON (*sniveling*): Mama, I didn't want to . . . It's all Plantin's fault! . . .

MOTHER: Plantin? You know someone with a name like Plantin?

AUDUBON: Léon Plantin, the Prime Minister . . .

MOTHER: I don't care if he's the Pope. His functions are immaterial. There is absolutely no excuse for you to hobnob with someone bearing such a terribly common name. You a Wilson, too!

AUDUBON: He's just been here. He made me drink, he practically forced me, then he bullied me into declaring war.

MOTHER: What! You agreed to declare war?

AUDUBON: He ordered me to, mama.

MOTHER: There are some orders one refuses to accept.

AUDUBON: There was nothing else I could do.

MOTHER: And it was this creature who made you drink this vile arak!

AUDUBON: Yes, mama. But I didn't want to, mama.

MOTHER: So this is the way you repay me for my kindness in allowing you to invite your friends here.

AUDUBON: But, mama, it's the government which . . .

MOTHER: The government! The government! You've been a very naughty boy, and as a punishment you shall not have that cake.

AUDUBON: Oh, mama, no . . .!

MOTHER: And may one ask what it's all about, this war that's going to get all your uniforms grubby once again?

AUDUBON: Oh, I won't go out very much, you know . . . it's the soldiers who will do the actual fighting . . .

MOTHER: Really, I can't leave you alone for five minutes without your getting into some kind of a scrape. Audubon, your behavior today has grieved me very much. You may receive your friends just this once, but another prank like this and you'll be very severely punished.

AUDUBON: Yes, mama. May I telephone my friends?

MOTHER: You may use the telephone if you wish. In my day a general would have sent his orderly to present a card.

AUDUBON: Oh, Robert would never do *that*. Besides, now I've got to send him out for some cookies.

MOTHER: You let that young man get away with anything. (*She leaves the room.*)

AUDUBON: Robert! Robert! (*Pause.*) How boring of mama to refuse to bake me a sponge cake. Now I shall have to buy cookies out of my allowance. (*He shrugs his shoulders.*) Drat! Oh, I've got an idea.

ROBERT *enters*.

Robert!

ROBERT: Yes, what is it now?

AUDUBON: Go down and buy half a pound of cookies. You know, those nice, cheap, round ones with a hole in the middle.

ROBERT: Very good, sir. Would you be good enough, sir, to give me some money for the purchase?

AUDUBON: Pay for them out of your own pocket! I'll settle with you later.

ROBERT: But I don't have any money, sir.

AUDUBON: What! You kept the change from the Prime Minister's thousand-franc note. I saw you!

ROBERT: I don't have it any longer . . . I left the money on the kitchen table and your ma took it.

AUDUBON: Well, really! You might at least have split it with me.

ROBERT: Yes. You're right, sir, it was absolutely rotten of me. If you wish, sir, I'll buy the cookies out of my savings.

AUDUBON: Oh, well, you don't have to . . .

ROBERT: Well, if you'd rather I didn't, sir . . .

AUDUBON: All right, if you insist. What a good idea. Off with you now, quickly.

ROBERT: Yes, sir.

AUDUBON (*alone*): That's how to retain the loyalty and affection of one's men. Ah! Now I must telephone my friends. (*He goes to the telephone.*) T . . . A . . . I . . . 5 . . . 4 . . . 3 . . . 9 . . . Hullo! Hullo! Hullo! Ah, is that you, d'Isigny? This is Wilson. Fine, thank you, and how are you? . . . Well, I simply wanted to ask you whether you'd care to come along to my place this afternoon . . . Oh, quite informal, you know, just few friends . . . a little tea party . . . Yes . . . Juillet, too . . . But of course. It will be nice to get to know some sailors . . . oh, he's in the Air Force . . . oh well, never mind . . . (*etc.*)

The curtain descends while he is still talking.

CURTAIN

Scene Two

This can take place in the same room, if preferred, or else in the Pétardières' dining room, in which case the room is repulsively bourgeois in appearance, with portraits of Zouaves hanging on the walls. As the curtain rises, AUDUBON *is fussing around the table, rearranging the dishes for the tea party and setting in the middle of the table an extremely unattractive vase of flowers. The doorbell rings.*

AUDUBON: Robert! Are you going to open the door?

ROBERT (*voice off-stage*): Yes, yes, I've only got one pair of legs.

> *Sound of voices. Enter General* DUPONT-D'ISIGNY, *escorted by* ROBERT, *who leaves again.*

DUPONT: My dear Wilson!

AUDUBON: My dear d'Isigny!

DUPONT: Dupont-d'Isigny. If it's not too much to ask, either address me by my full name or else don't mention my name at all and don't even speak to me.

AUDUBON: Oh, but I assure you, I had no intention . . .

DUPONT (*coldly*): It's really of no importance. (*He looks around him.*) What a charming place you have here. Delightfully arranged.

AUDUBON: Do you think so?

DUPONT (*aside*): How ghastly.

AUDUBON: My mother looks after everything absolutely marvelously. She's so self-sacrificing.

DUPONT: Ah! Mothers! The true companions of warriors like us.

AUDUBON: How right you are. A profound thought, that, you know, yet without appearing to be so.

DUPONT: On the contrary, I think it *does* appear profound . . . I've been having a great deal of success with that phrase for five months now. I thought it up . . . let me see . . . (*counts on his fingers*) last January. . . . So you see! It's been thoroughly tested!

AUDUBON (*admiringly*): Five months of success with one phrase, that's really something! But do sit down. How about a nip of anisette?

DUPONT: Wouldn't it be more polite to wait for the others?

AUDUBON: Oh, all right.

They both listen.

Eh . . . No . . .

Doorbell rings.

Yes!

TOGETHER: There they are!

Enter Generals LAVESTE *and* JUILLET, *escorted by* ROBERT, *who leaves again.*

AUDUBON: My dear friends! . . . Right on time!

DUPONT (*sourly*): So I was early, I suppose!

LAVESTE: No, no, it is we who are late.

AUDUBON: Really, Dupont, old fellow, you *are* touchy.

DUPONT: My name is Dupont-d'Isigny (*accentuating the D's*) if you don't mind.

LAVESTE: Lenvers de Laveste! Delighted to meet you.

JUILLET: Juillet! Charmed.

Handshakes all around.

AUDUBON: Well, here we all are then! Let's have tea right away, shall we? Do sit down! . . . Don't stand on ceremony, now. Just sit where you like.

DUPONT (*shouts*): Sit down.

Everybody sits down.

JUILLET: Mmm! Look at all these delicious things to eat!

AUDUBON: And mama *did* bake a sponge cake for me after all. Oh, but goodness, I had a time persuading her. She was so vexed with me, you know: she caught me in the act of drinking a glass of Pernod . . . (*He laughs, rather proud of himself.*) So I had to put the anisette in the teapot. Hah! . . . What a rascal I am.

LAVESTE: Oh, very naughty indeed! (*To* JUILLET, *in an undertone:*) Is he a complete moron?

JUILLET (*also in an undertone*): Well, I suppose he has some good points. (*Aloud.*) But you brought us all along to tell us some great piece of news, didn't you, my dear Audubon? Am I being premature in asking what it is?

AUDUBON: Oh, let's have tea first. I'll be mother.

DUPONT: But we are burning with impatience.

LAVESTE: How interesting. You say "burning" whereas *I* say "boiling."

DUPONT: Boiling what?

LAVESTE: I say *boiling* with impatience.

JUILLET: That's funny: I always say *consumed* with impatience.

AUDUBON: Well, burning is what happens when one cooks under the grill, boiling is the opposite when everything turns soggy in water, and in either case the food gets consumed anyway.

DUPONT (*bewildered, aside*): I don't understand a word of all this! The man's a half-wit.

JUILLET: The fact remains, my dear Audubon, that I'm eating my heart out in impatience.

LAVESTE: So now you're eating yourself!

JUILLET: Damn it, this culinary discussion is making me feel quite hungry.

AUDUBON: Listen, before we get down to business, let's have a good old gossip, shall we? We see each other so seldom, let's take this opportunity of getting to know each other better. After all, this is the first time that the whole G.H.Q. has ever got together. To start with, we should all call each other by our first names, don't you think: it's so much cozier, isn't it! (*To* LAVESTE:) What's your first name, Laveste?

LAVESTE: Michel.

AUDUBON: Oh, what a charming name.

JUILLET: Charming—charming!

LAVESTE (*shyly*): He's the patron saint of warriors.

AUDUBON: Hmm, yes, a pity about that, but it's still a charming name. (*To* JUILLET:) And you, my dear?

JUILLET (*gloomily*): Philippe.

ALL: Ah!

Everyone rises.

ALL (*in unison*): All honor to courage in misfortune!

They sit down again.

LAVESTE (*nostalgically*): Ah! To think that there was a time when you could still hope to earn a Field Marshal's seven stars without ending up in jail! . . .

JUILLET: Yes, they ration our stars, yet the humblest pair of lovers can look up into the night sky and reach down all the stars they want.

ALL (*together*): Oh, how sublime!—What a delicious analogy!—What a poet!

JUILLET: Oh, that's nothing. For six years now I've been translating the military training manual into Greek alexandrines, so you see . . .

AUDUBON: My dear Philippe, if I tell you that your oak leaves are intertwined with a plangent lute string, I think I shall only be expressing the . . . general . . . opinion. (*He laughs.*)

ALL (*together*): Exquisite— How appropriate— What a wit!

AUDUBON: You are too kind. (*To* DUPONT:) How about you, my dear Dupont . . .

AUDUBON *and* DUPONT (*together*): d'Isigny.

AUDUBON: What's your first name?

DUPONT: Hmm! . . . I can't stand my first name . . . It's Georges.

LAVESTE: Ha! St. George and the Dragoons! . . .

AUDUBON: Yes, you certainly have plenty of men under you!

DUPONT: Not enough for my taste: I'm ambitious. (*He laughs.*) Oh, I admit it, that's part of my charm. But, you know, I had an absolutely mad idea once: I wanted to call myself God.

Frozen silence, accompanied by expressions that are respectively distant, contemptuous, and embarrassed.

AUDUBON: Well, really, Dupont . . .

LAVESTE: Aren't you going a bit far?

JUILLET: Yes, I mean we aren't butchers, after all.

DUPONT (*annoyed*): Oh, all right, I won't say another word.

AUDUBON: Come, come, don't let's start quarreling. (*He passes the cookies around.*) Let's have a little snack.

Crunching noises mingled with noises of glasses being filled.

Anisette, Michel? Anisette, Philippe?

LAVESTE *and* JUILLET (*together*): Yes, please— By all means.

AUDUBON: Georges? Come on, take a drink with us, don't look so glum.

DUPONT (*sulkily*): I'm not looking glum. I'm sulking.

JUILLET: Cheer up, everybody. Listen, I know an amusing riddle. It'll cheer you all up. (*To* AUDUBON:) Shall I ask it?

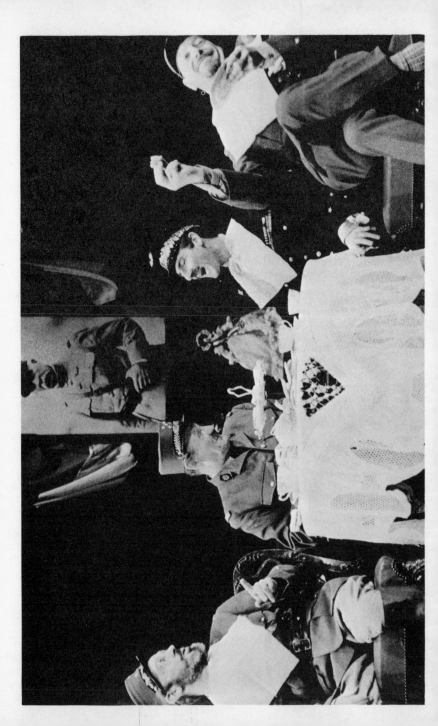

AUDUBON: So long as it's decent.

JUILLET: Oh, of course. (*Giggles.*) But it'll make you rack your brains!

LAVESTE: Oh, go on then, ask us.

JUILLET: I'd like to, but I don't want to offend anybody.

AUDUBON: My dear friend, if it's a decent riddle, we'll be only too delighted to hear you ask it . . . !

JUILLET: Oh, I feel quite upset now, you've made me feel silly.

AUDUBON *and* LAVESTE (*together*): Go on, ask us—come on, be a sport.

DUPONT (*icily*): He's taking you for a ride.

JUILLET: Well, all right then. You've got to guess a five-letter word starting with M and ending with E, and an R in the middle, which recalls the memory of a great general.

Icy silence.

Oh! Now I feel quite embarrassed . . . !

Loud guffaw from DUPONT.

AUDUBON: Hmm . . . my dear fellow . . . really . . . I know you have a racy sense of humor, but there are . . . heh! heh! . . . speed limits, you know . . .

JUILLET (*angrily*): Oh damn it, I didn't want to tell you the riddle anyway. I knew you wouldn't appreciate it. Well, if you want to know, the answer is M-A-R-N-E, Marne, the great victory of General Joffre.

LAVESTE: Ha, *merde* . . . I mean, marvelous! What an absolutely delightful riddle!

DUPONT (*admiringly*): He's certainly taken us for a ride all right—in taxis!

Everyone bursts out laughing, while DUPONT *smirks.*

AUDUBON: Remarkable, my dear friend, remarkable. And in such exquisite taste . . . Here, Juillet, have a little more anisette, your glass is empty.

JUILLET: Thanks. (*Drinks.*)

AUDUBON (*to the others*): A cookie, anyone? Another drop of anisette? Georges? No? Michel? Won't you really?

ALL (*together*): Had enough . . . No, thanks . . . Absolutely full . . .

AUDUBON (*lays down his napkin and pushes back his chair*): Well then, now that we've all taken refreshment, let's get down to a serious talk.

JUILLET: At last!

LAVESTE: I was simply dying of impatience!

DUPONT: Oh dear, are you dying?

JUILLET: He's dying! How peculiar!

AUDUBON: The fact is . . .

Silence, while he hesitates.

. . . that Léon Plantin has just left here.

DUPONT (*dryly*): I must say, you have some queer friends.

AUDUBON: I can't help it: after all, he *is* the Prime Minister at the moment.

JUILLET (*airily*): Hah! Not for much longer, I'll bet.

AUDUBON: I rather agree with you, especially after what he has just suggested to me. (*He giggles.*) Oh yes, he's for the high jump all right. The fact of the matter is: Léon Plantin wants a war.

All jump to their feet.

ALL (*together*): He must be mad!

AUDUBON: Well, yes, quite batty, but there you are.

DUPONT: It's a good thing we had our little snack before-hand.

LAVESTE: Yes, indeed. A dreadful piece of news like that would have absolutely ruined my appetite. Did he explain *why* he wanted a war?

AUDUBON: Are you kidding? He just talked a lot of old rubbish—something to do with the fact that hardware isn't selling very well, as far as I could make out.

LAVESTE: Bah! That's ridiculous, why can't he sell something else instead?

AUDUBON: Apparently everything else is selling just as badly.

JUILLET: Ah, that's going too far, it's always we generals who have to pay the piper. Your pal Plantin is really playing with fire.

AUDUBON: Hmm! I gather that coal isn't selling too well, either.

LAVESTE: This is all very annoying, you know; nothing disorganizes an army so much as war.

JUILLET: Could we perhaps just have a very short war?

AUDUBON: Plantin would be furious. And then, with a short war, you know, we'd still be saddled with a lot of firebrands who've been promoted over our heads. No, if we've got to have a war, let's have a really good one. Oh, you know, I did everything in my power to bring him to his senses.

DUPONT: The whole thing's out of the question, in any case. Look here, you'd better get on the phone right away and talk him out of it.

AUDUBON: Not a hope in hell. He's dead set on the whole project. In fact, I'd advise you to steer clear of him if you want to save yourselves from being bored to death by completely idiotic economic theories . . . I didn't understand a single word, myself.

JUILLET: I say no! No war!

LAVESTE: No war!

DUPONT: I agree. No war!

AUDUBON (*getting up*): Gentlemen, it's an order.

Deadly silence.

JUILLET: You take full responsibility?

AUDUBON: Yes.

LAVESTE: Oh well, in that case, of course, I agree.

Murmurs of agreement all around.

Still, it's really very tiresome. Give me a drop of anisette. I feel quite upset.

AUDUBON (*in a conspiratorial voice*): I've got something better than that. Pernod! (*He gets up and goes to fetch the bottle.*)

JUILLET: Oh, what a good idea!

DUPONT: My dear Wilson, you seem to be making progress. (*He laughs mockingly.*) Two or three more wars and you'll turn into a real soldier!

AUDUBON: Sarcastic, as always! (*Pours drinks all around.*) Enough water? Say when!

The others all indicate in turn when their glasses are full enough. AUDUBON *pours himself a drink and sits down again.*

Gentlemen, I have a favor to ask of you: don't say a word about this to my mother.

JUILLET: About the war? Of course not!

AUDUBON: No, not the war, that doesn't matter, and in any case I'll have to discuss that with her eventually—I mean about the Pernod. (*Pointing.*) She has forbidden me to drink. (*Brightening up.*) But I drink in secret. I'm a real devil, aren't I?

DUPONT (*aside*): I'm wrong about him. Not a half-wit, a complete idiot.

LAVESTE: But tell me, have you made all the arrangements?

AUDUBON: Euh . . . the actual details, yes, well, that's up to you three. We'll have a general discussion later on . . . One question occurs to me immediately, in fact: on what can we count?

DUPONT: What do you mean, on "what"?

AUDUBON: Well, yes, on what—on what resources, on what . . . oh, I don't know: I mean, how many divisions have you got in *your* army?

DUPONT: Hmm . . . you know, a division tends to be rather an elastic unit . . . as far as I'm concerned . . . hmm . . . Oh, I must have something between two and nine divisions . . . but, at the moment, what with the holidays, deferred service, the Tour de France and so on, I'd be surprised if the strength amounted to twelve thousand men.

AUDUBON: Each division?

DUPONT: No, no! *In toto*.

AUDUBON: Tchk! tchk! that's not much. Ah well . . . I suppose we can figure it all out between now and then.

DUPONT: When is "then," may one ask?

AUDUBON: Oh, I don't know, that's up to you, isn't it? You are the G.H.Q. after all. In any case, as soon as possible, Plantin said.

LAVESTE: Are the posters ready?

JUILLET: What posters?

LAVESTE: The mobilization posters.

AUDUBON: Oh dear, yes! The posters! We simply must have some posters. What a nuisance. Oh, there must be *some* left over from 1939.

DUPONT: Posters are absolutely necessary. "Your country needs *you*."

JUILLET: Yes, but those mobilization posters only rake in a bunch of amateurs.

LAVESTE: Oh, what a damn nuisance this war is. Give me another Pernod.

AUDUBON (*to* LAVESTE): How about you, Laveste, what have you got available at the moment?

LAVESTE: Oh, don't worry about me, I'll get by. And after all, aircraft are not all that important, are they?

AUDUBON: I quite agree. Whatever people may say, it's the infantry that counts. An infantryman's mug is a beautiful sight to behold, by God! Oh, what am I saying! (*He takes the bottle.*) Hey, another round, you chaps?

Various answers of agreement.

(*To* JUILLET:) You, Juillet, how are your tanks?

JUILLET: My tanks? (*Cynical laugh.*) Oh, very well, thank you. Just the same as ever. All covered in rust.

AUDUBON: What, they are still the same ones?

JUILLET: Yes, the American ones we scraped off the beaches in 1945. We have got a few prototypes of new models, of course, but we are not developing those until we find out what the other countries are up to. In any case, there's not a tank today which can stand up to the latest anti-tank weapons, so what's the point of building them? The old ones will be quite good enough for our purposes—no point in wasting money. But it's the industrialists who make all the decisions in these matters; we'll work it out with them.

AUDUBON (*optimistically*): So you'd say that things are no worse than usual?

DUPONT: Certainly. I'd go so far as to say that things are as good as usual.

AUDUBON: Besides, it's the training that really counts, don't you agree? In the end, it's the infantry which decides the outcome of wars, and thank God, our French sergeant majors are the envy of military establishments throughout the world. (*He rubs his hands together.*) Well, now that we have got down to the root of the problem, we should consider a few details. For instance, we may have a bit of trouble arousing the public's enthusiasm. With all these wars we've been having lately, people are becoming rather bored with the idea. We've just got to think up some really original gimmick. What's the word I'm looking for? . . . Euh . . . yes, propaganda, that's what we need—propaganda.

JUILLET: Well, we can count on the journalists for that, they always support us. They have always reserved their largest headlines for us. The bigger the headline the fewer words they have to write underneath it.

AUDUBON: Yes, yes, I know, but the trouble is that nobody reads them. And they are all liars anyway. No, when I say propaganda I don't mean newspapers—that's just paid publicity. We've got to try to get ordinary people interested in making propaganda . . . surely there must be something we can do about that.

DUPONT: To start with, I think we're faced with one absolutely basic problem, and I'd like to know if you all agree with me about it. Here it is. I think it is quite essential that we should have the Archbishop and his gang on our side.

LAVESTE: Ah ha! Yes, I think you've put your finger on it.

JUILLET: Oh, absolutely essential.

DUPONT: Yes, how right you are, after all they are really the only group left which commands a certain credit.

They have so much more money than anyone else that no one can accuse them of having sold out to the Government. They would be more likely to have bought up the Government outright. Oh yes, the public really looks up to the Church. Believe me, I've been through a few wars, and I tell you that if the Archbishop marches with us we've as good as won already.

LAVESTE: Couldn't we ask him to join our tea party? Do you know the Archbishop well?

AUDUBON (*looking at his watch*): Patience, gentlemen, I'm glad you asked me that. I have already invited the Archbishop to join our conference. But he had to go out shopping: a perfectly ridiculous expedition, incidentally. Can you imagine, he says it's just impossible at the moment to buy purple socks in the ecclesiastical outfitters around the Place Saint-Sulpice because the teenagers from Saint-Germain-des-Prés have bought them all up . . . so poor old Roland had to go all the way to Versailles to hunt a pair down. He should be here now . . . in fact, he's already five minutes late according to my calculations . . . I wanted to give you a surprise. (*He gets up and goes to the door.*) I'll go and have a look.

DUPONT (*aside*): The biggest driveling idiot I've ever come across. One has to take one's hat off to him.

LAVESTE (*to* JUILLET): What do you think about all this?

JUILLET (*pointing toward* AUDUBON): So long as he's assuming all responsibility, I couldn't care less.

DUPONT: Yes, it's his war, isn't it; nothing to do with us at all.

LAVESTE: Still, in these days there is a certain risk attached. Think of poor Rommel.

JUILLET: Well, yes, I agree, the whole thing's an awful bore, but what chance is there of knocking sense into that stupid bastard Plantin.

LAVESTE: There's no doubt about it, civilian conscription absolutely ruins the armed forces.

DUPONT: Let's face it, Plantin is taking very serious risks.

JUILLET: Balls! Anybody can take serious risks when they are other people's risks.

LAVESTE: What the hell! We're stuck with it, I suppose.

JUILLET: I still feel sure that Audubon will find some way out for all of us. In any case, my dear Dupont, that was a clever idea of yours about the Archbishop.

DUPONT: Thank you, but Audubon hit on the idea first, so it can't be that clever, can it—and by the way, may I remind you that my name is Dupont-d'Isigny.

LAVESTE: Oh it's a clever idea all right. But I still can't get Rommel out of my mind. A morbid feeling. I was very upset at the time.

DUPONT: Sheer neurosis! Listen, you'd better see my psychiatrist, a marvelous man. He cured my complexes in no time at all.

AUDUBON (*coming back*): He can't be much longer. (*To* DUPONT:) What's that I hear, my dear friend—you, a soldier, have complexes?

DUPONT: A terrible complex. I mean, really, I became quite neurotic. Oh, it's silly, I know. But one lets oneself get influenced. The fact remains that being a homosexual caused me a great deal of pain.

AUDUBON: Oh yes? A great deal of pain? I'm so sorry. Where exactly did you feel the pain?

DUPONT: Well, I was embarrassed. Whenever I ran across a plumber's mate in the street I used to blush all over—yes, it was always plumbers' mates that affected me like that. But why, I'd like to know. To plumb the depths of the soul of a career soldier . . . an insoluble task, you might think. But my psychiatrist actually succeeded. Today I am completely cured.

JUILLET: Well, I'm glad to hear that!

DUPONT: Yes, I'm no longer in the least ashamed of being a homosexual. It all seems perfectly normal to me.

Loud ringing noise.

LAVESTE: Someone's ringing!

AUDUBON: Yes, it must be Roland! I'll go and see. (*He trots off.*)

JUILLET: There is something reassuring about the sheer animal vigor of that episcopal finger pressed against the doorbell.

Sound of Audubon's voice, yelling angrily at ROBERT.

AUDUBON (*voice off-stage*): You imbecile, why did you have to do that at this particular moment? (*He returns.*)

That cretin Robert was testing his alarm clock.

DUPONT: What an extraordinary idea! (*Aside.*) They really are all complete idiots in this household.

Sound of thunderous banging on the door.

ROBERT (*voice off-stage*): I'll see to it, guv.

AUDUBON: Well, I'm certainly not getting up this time.

Enter Monseigneur ROLAND TAPECUL.

DUPONT: I beg your pardon.

ROLAND: Really! Your manservant! What a dimwit.

AUDUBON (*rising*): Roland! At last . . . Allow me to introduce you to my G.H.Q. Laveste. Juillet. D'Isigny.

DUPONT: General Dupont-d'Isigny, if you don't mind . . .

AUDUBON: General Dupont-d'Isigny, excuse me, dear friend . . . or, to be more exact, Philippe Dupont-d'Isigny.

JUILLET: No, no, *I'm* Philippe!

ALL (*rising and chanting in unison*): All honor to courage in misfortune.

AUDUBON (*throwing his arm around Roland's shoulder*): And this is Monseigneur Roland Tapecul, my old school chum.

ROLAND (*imitation of Texas accent and gesture*): Friends, just call me Roland. (*He sits down.*) What are you all drinking?

AUDUBON: Pernod.

ROLAND: Splendid! Deal me in.

AUDUBON *serves him.*

AUDUBON: Who wants a refill? Come on, we don't have a party every day.

All hands are outstretched, clutching glasses.

ROLAND (*drinking*): Mmm! Just what I needed. Jesus, Versailles sure is a hell of a long way off.

JUILLET: Monseigneur! Surely you went by car?

ROLAND: None of this Monseigneur business, just Roland

please. Yes, of course I went by car, but the arch-diocese's official chauffeur drives like he was conducting a hearse.

LAVESTE: What kind of a car have you got?

ROLAND: Oh, a Cadillac. Personally, I would have preferred a more compact automobile, but the difficulty was getting my crozier inside. In any case, you know, we archbishops have to make do with what we are offered.

JUILLET: With a Cadillac, it shouldn't take you long to get to Versailles.

ROLAND: But my chauffeur is a complete numskull, I tell you. He spends his time carting nuns around, and every time he gets to a street crossing he stops for all the old ladies. My God.

DUPONT: Well, anyhow, here you are, so can we perhaps get down to a serious discussion?

AUDUBON: Yes, we asked you around because these gentle-men and I have a . . . hmm . . . little plan that we are working out, and we'd like your advice.

ROLAND: You do me too much honor, my children. Is my opinion really so important?

AUDUBON: Well, actually, well what we really need is your agreement. Look, it's no good beating about the pul-pit—Léon Plantin wants a war.

ROLAND: Sure, we all know that. He's a nut on that subject.

AUDUBON: But this time he really means it. And he wants this war right away too. And naturally all the hard work will fall on me.

ROLAND: My heart bleeds for you, pardner . . . But that's the way the cookie crumbles.

AUDUBON: However, since I suppose I shall have to make the best of a bad job, I want at least to have a few trumps up my sleeve. Which is why I asked you to come along. To come to the point: what is the Pope's present position?

JUILLET (*looking at his watch*): Probably on his knees praying, I should think.

ROLAND: The position of Pius? Pious, of course. But you mean the position of the Church? Crystal clear, as always. We simply have to take into consideration the fact that one side constitutes a good cause, while the other side constitutes a bad cause.

DUPONT: Hmm! Yes, for once its position is indeed perfectly clear.

ROLAND: We uphold the thesis that the good cause should triumph.

LAVESTE: Ah, naturally.

JUILLET: Brilliantly put.

DUPONT: Perfectly clear.

AUDUBON: Well, that solves the whole problem . . .

A silence.

Hmm! But . . . how do you recognize which is the good cause?

ROLAND: Because it triumphs, of course!

JUILLET (*enthusiastically*): Oh! How sublime!

ROLAND: Whoah, there! (*He sips his drink.*) Experience shows that it is important not to confuse an apparent triumph with a real triumph.

LAVESTE (*disappointed*): But then . . . the problem arises once more . . . How is one to distinguish between these two categories of triumph?

ROLAND (*touching the tip of his nose*): Follow your nose.

AUDUBON: I beg your pardon?

ROLAND: It's a question of sniffing the wind. Follow your nose, as they say, and you can't go wrong.

AUDUBON: Well, that seems rather risky.

ROLAND: Oh, not really. After five or six years it's usually possible to tell which is the genuine victor. By then, even if one has chosen wrong, one can always make the excuse that conditions are no longer the same. . . . But in any case, I'm no expert, you know, you'd do better to ask the Cardinal.

AUDUBON: To get back to my original question, what will the Pope's attitude be?

ROLAND: Here's my advice to you: just get on with your war, and you'll find that things will work out fine. In any case, I'll support you to start with. If they put the screws on His Holiness, he'll simply read me out of the party . . . and so what? That still wouldn't stop me from becoming a cardinal. The Church is not responsible for human error . . .

AUDUBON: Roland, you're a real pal. I knew you'd stick up for me.

ROLAND: Oh, don't be a slob. Get me a drink, you old fossil.

AUDUBON: Hey! Don't call me names like that. One moment you're being perfectly sweet and the next moment you're insulting me.

ROLAND: Not at all, a dandy description—you should have chosen a different profession.

AUDUBON: Well, in that case—down with the God-botherers!

ROLAND (*laughs loudly*): What a moron!

DUPONT (*aside, to* ROLAND): He really embarrasses me, I must say.

ROLAND: Instead of making an ass out of yourself, you'd do better to concentrate your mind, such as it is, on the war: surely you are faced with a few details which need working out. What's the situation?

AUDUBON: Well, euh . . . what situation?

ROLAND: Everything, doggone it! Or has the Military Intelligence Department shut up shop?

AUDUBON: Laveste is the man responsible for that gang. He'll be able to put you in the picture.

ROLAND (*to* LAVESTE): Well, go on, give me the lowdown, then!

LAVESTE: Oh, everything's very calm, very calm; nothing particularly exciting happening at the moment.

ROLAND: But you must know *something*! What's the inside dope?

LAVESTE: Well, for instance . . . did you know that Admiral Floraline is wearing a pair of horns in his cocked hat —courtesy of his wife?

AUDUBON: Laveste! Supposing my mother came in . . . Please moderate your language!

LAVESTE: Sorry. I'm so used to using technical expressions . . . But you must admit it's amusing.

ROLAND: Yes indeed. Floraline . . . ha! That's a real gas! A case of the biter bit, of course. Come on now, with your network of agents you must have been able to scrape up some more dirt. Is it true, for instance, that Plantin has been screwing Molleton's daughter?

LAVESTE: Yes, but everybody knows that. The papers have it listed in the entertainment columns.

ROLAND: What a splendid job you have: all those secrets just waiting to be dug out!

LAVESTE: Well, you people have pretty good facilities yourselves.

ROLAND: Oh, the confessional isn't the same thing at all. People come up to us to tell us things on purpose . . . it lacks the charm of forbidden fruit. But tell me more. How about the Minister of Agriculture? Are the rumors about his sexual habits true?

LAVESTE: Afraid I don't know—are they? You must realize that I do my work as discreetly as possible . . . and, anyhow, listening at keyholes gives me the earache.

ROLAND: Ah, but it's such good sport. And so harmless.

LAVESTE: It might be if I did it myself—but my agents keep all the best bits for themselves.

AUDUBON: Hmm . . . My dear friends, I think we are straying rather far from the subject.

ROLAND: Stop blushing, you old virgin . . .

AUDUBON: Roland, really!

DUPONT: Come now, Audubon, Roland was only having a little joke. (*Aside.*) What a miserable specimen!

AUDUBON: No, he wasn't joking. I know him, he has always teased me. Even at school he was a nasty bully, and he's just as rotten now.

JUILLET: Come, come, let's all have a drink and stop squabbling: everybody kiss and make up.

AUDUBON: Ah no! I refuse to kiss him!

ROLAND: What a sourpuss you are. Stop being pigheaded now, and come over and kiss me immediately.

AUDUBON (*sulky and pouting*): No! (*But he gets up and shuffles reluctantly and sheepishly toward* ROLAND.)

ROLAND: All is forgiven. (*Kisses* AUDUBON *on both cheeks.*) There, you old fossil.

AUDUBON *mumbles something indistinct.*

What?

AUDUBON *does same business.*

(*Horrified:*) Oh! . . . Oh! . . . Really! Now you've gone too far, Audubon, you should be ashamed of yourself.

AUDUBON (*goes and sits down again, looking vaguely pleased with himself*): That'll teach you.

JUILLET: What did he say?

ROLAND: Oh, the filthy beast. He said: "Up your shiter with your mitre!"

DUPONT: Heh, heh! . . . that's not bad! . . .

LAVESTE: Hmm . . . it will pass.

AUDUBON *triumphantly thumbs his nose at* ROLAND.

ROLAND: You're a fine bunch of bums. I've a good mind to. . .

AUDUBON (*hastily*): No violence, please! My mother might come in. (*He draws himself up.*) Perhaps we had better take a little break, since everybody's attention seems to be wandering. But first, to get back to the original question: are you on our side?

ROLAND: Look, I've already answered that. Of course we are on your side. What a damn fool question.

AUDUBON: Well, that solves the main problem. We can start work on the details tomorrow.

JUILLET (*getting up*): Gentlemen, there is still a most vital matter to be settled. (*Bangs the table with his fist.*)

ALL (*together, nervously*): What?—you frightened me— Juillet, what's up?

JUILLET: Whom shall we choose to accompany us as patron saint?

LAVESTE: Ah! Yes!

DUPONT: Of course! Hmm, that's quite a problem!

ROLAND: Yes indeed, that does present certain difficulties. Let's see. (*Counting on his fingers.*) How about St. Aphasia?

JUILLET: Raped to death, 702.

DUPONT: No. She's been used too often.

ROLAND: St. Joan of Arc?

JUILLET: Burned at the stake, 1431.

LAVESTE: Ah no, that's a cooked-up story.

ROLAND: Well, how about St. Lawrence, then?

JUILLET: Broiled to death, 258.

DUPONT: St. Lawrence? No, no. A mere flash in the pan.

AUDUBON: Ha! I've got it! An inspired idea.

ALL (*together*): Who?—What?—Go on, tell us!

AUDUBON (*rising*): St. Philip.

ALL (*rising*): All honor to courage in misfortune!

ROLAND (*impatiently*): St. Philip? Let's see . . . hmm . . .
that seems fine, but what the devil did he do?

DUPONT: Come now, Roland! Think.

ROLAND (*impatiently*): Yes, yes, of course I know about
him, but I mean the other St. Philip, the real one?

DUPONT: Were there two?

JUILLET (*intoning*): To start off with, there are three of
them: St. Philip the apostle who was born in Beth-
saida, preached in Phrygia and died crucified upside
down in the year 80 for having opposed snake worship.
His feast day used to be May 1st before that particular
day became consecrated to the performance of a most
regrettable annual ritual . . . which we all have to
suffer in silence. Then there is St. Philip, Bishop of
Heraclea, burned at the stake at Adrianople on Octo-
ber 22nd 304 by order of the priest Severus, and the
deacon Hermes. Lastly, there is St. Philip Diaconus,
who was born in Caesarea, baptized Queen Candace's
eunuch, preached in Samaria, and died in December

of the year 70. And mark this, his feast day is June 6th!

LAVESTE: June 6th! Ah, that strikes a chord! Now what else was it that happened on that day once? (*Thinks hard, brightens suddenly and says:*)1789! Declaration of the Rights of Man! (*Then crestfallen.*) Ah, no, that was the Night of August 4th. Hmm! . . . June 6th . . . Let me think . . .

ROLAND (*to* LAVESTE): The Normandy Landing, you fool! (*To* JUILLET:) My congratulations. You know all that stuff backwards. Which of them shall we choose, then?

DUPONT: The Bishop of Heraclea. He was burned alive, so he is now fireproof. He can be appointed patron saint of the flame-thrower units.

AUDUBON: Very good, Juillet, I'll see that the Tunisian government awards you the Order of the Nicham-Iftikar.

JUILLET: Thanks, but I already have eleven of them. . . . Roland, do you know what I'd really like? Not that I really believe in all that stuff, but still—would you please give us your blessing?

ROLAND: Oh, for chrissake! . . . I mean, sure, I'd be glad to, but you make rather a small congregation, don't you. Say, why don't we simply make the scene over at a swinging little joint I know near Saint-Sulpice? It's called the Double Cross. We always go there after staging one of those real ritzy shows at the Cathedral.

AUDUBON: No, no, here, please. A blessing, and Robert will take a photo! (*Calls out:*) Robert!

ROBERT (*voice off-stage*): Yes, sir, I'm coming. (*Enters.*)

AUDUBON: Robert, bring in all the equipment, we are going to have a photo of us all being blessed.

ROBERT: Right away, guv. (*He goes out, comes back laden with photographic equipment, etc., goes out again.*)

AUDUBON (*calls out*): I'll get some music! (*To the others:*) All of you over here!

    ROBERT *pushes a harmonium into the room.*

Yes, we can all pose as Cranach's Angel Musicians.

LAVESTE: Hey, may I play the kazoo? I'm marvelous on the kazoo . . . !

AUDUBON: No, no, this is a choir with organ prelude. (*He sits down at the harmonium and plays a prelude.*)

    ROBERT *re-enters with more photographic apparatus and starts setting it all up. All strike up heroic poses.*

Right, now! One, two, three . . .

CHORUS: Save, sa-a-a-ave Europe
            In the name of the Sacred Heart.

Flashbulb.

ROBERT: Very good! One more, please. Lift your nose, general! No, not you! Dupont!

DUPONT: D'Isigny! Dupont d'Isigny, please.

ROBERT: Shut up! Right, hold your poses. Music!

CHORUS: Save, sa-a-a-ave Europe
            In the name of the Sacred Heart.

JUILLET (*ecstatically*): Ah! What sublime music!

    Enter MME. DE LA PETARDIERE. *Total silence.*

MOTHER: Well, well, the youngsters seem to be enjoying their music lessons! (*To her son:*) Introduce your playmates to me, Audubon.

AUDUBON: Yes, mama. (*Introducing them in turn.*) You know Roland. This is Georges, this is Michel and this is Philippe.

ALL (*in unison*): Good afternoon, Madame. (*They go up to* MME. DE LA PETARDIERE *one after the other, to kiss her hand politely.*)

MOTHER: Well, did you enjoy my sponge cake?

DUPONT: Oh yes, Madame.

ROLAND: The greatest.

LAVESTE: Excellent.

JUILLET: Delicious, absolutely delicious.

MOTHER: Carry on with your games, children. What were you up to just as I came in?

AUDUBON: Euh, well . . . we were having a little concert, mama.

ROLAND: Pardon me, ma'am. (*To* AUDUBON:) I've got to beat it.

DUPONT: Yes, me too.

LAVESTE: I really ought to go home too. My wife is alone looking after my dad.

JUILLET: I'll come with you. I have to be at the Etoile at six o'clock.

AUDUBON: Oh! Are you all going?

MOTHER: I hope you are not leaving on my account? (*Said in a tone of voice which makes it clear that she hopes exactly that.*)

ALL (*protesting*): Certainly not—ah, no—my dear lady . . . !

—Of course not. (*They all go up to her and say good-by politely but sullenly. But their good humor returns as they make their farewells to* AUDUBON. *The last one to do so,* ROLAND, *gives him a resounding slap on the cheek.*)

ROLAND: Good-by, you old fossil—see you soon.

The MOTHER *glares at them as they leave the room.* AUDUBON *leaves the room for a moment, then returns, to find his* MOTHER *sniffing the glasses.*

MOTHER: So, did you enjoy yourselves?

AUDUBON: Oh yes, we played games and had a good old gossip.

MOTHER: Audubon, you've been drinking again!

AUDUBON: Mother, I promise you I haven't! It's the others.

MOTHER: I've just smelled your glass.

AUDUBON: But it wasn't I who drank out of it. I haven't drunk a drop.

MOTHER: You are lying, of course. However, I won't insist. Obviously, if you go around with a degenerate like that archbishop your moral character is bound to suffer.

AUDUBON: But he's an old schoolmate of mine, mama . . .

MOTHER: Then I'm sorry for the sake of the reputation of a school such as the Lycée Janson de Sailly, which was in my time considered highly respectable. I forbid you to see this boy again—he can only have a bad influence on you.

AUDUBON: But . . . but . . . in my profession, you know, I simply have to have certain contacts . . .

MOTHER: Ha, yes! Like that disgusting man Plantin! I really wonder where on earth you find these people.

AUDUBON: But, mama . . .

MOTHER: I'll bet you've been playing war games again.

AUDUBON *looks down guiltily.*

Yes, I knew. Whose idea was it?

AUDUBON: Plantin's, mama. And everyone else agreed.

MOTHER: Of course! He's a thoroughly nasty specimen, your friend Plantin. Against whom, may I ask, do you propose to wage this war?

AUDUBON: Against whom? (*The question suddenly sinks in.*) Against whom! My God! That's true.

MOTHER (*shriek of horror*): Oh! Audubon! Swearing in my presence! You must be out of your mind! I'll deal with you later, you naughty boy. (*She leaves the room.*)

AUDUBON (*paying no attention to this last speech, rushes to the telephone*): Hullo! Hullo! (*He replaces the receiver and dials again.*) Hullo! Damn! Damn! Hullo! Léon Plantin, please! A personal call . . . General Audubon Wilson de la Pétardière-Frenouillou . . . Yes . . . I tell you it's a personal call. Goddamn it, man, will you get me Plantin on the line . . . Yes . . . Plantin . . . What? Are you trying to tell me you are the grain-merchants Vilmorin-Andrieux? I want to speak to the Prime Minister. . . . What? . . . Coffins? . . . You sell coffins? What number am I speaking to? (*Silence.*) Oh hell! (*He redials, grumbling.*) I'm getting nervous. Must calm down . . . (*He dials the number slowly.*) E . . . L . . . Y . . . zero . . . zero . . . one . . . nine . . . Hullo! . . . Elysée zero zero one nine?

At last. This is General Audubon James Wilson de la Pétardière-Frenouillou. What's the initial? Are you trying to suggest that there's someone else of the same name? . . . Hullo . . . Get me Léon Plantin . . . The Prime Minister. . . . What? . . He isn't Prime Minister any longer? . . . Oh, you were joking, were you? . . . Well, listen, my friend, it was a damn silly joke . . . Hullo . . . Plantin? Yes . . . This is Audubon . . . Yes . . . Listen, old boy, we've forgotten something. . . . This war of yours: whom are we supposed to be fighting? . . . What? . . . I am *not* asking ridiculous questions, I'm asking you a most vital question. . . . We should have thought about that beforehand? Listen, it's our job to make war, not to choose the enemy. That's your business, I believe . . . Are you or are you not the Foreign Minister? . . . Oh, so you don't give a damn whether you are or not. Well, nor do I, for that matter . . . All right then . . . We must get this settled right away . . . Tomorrow morning? Yes, certainly . . . Don't forget to warn Korkiloff, Jackson, and Ching Ping Ting to come along . . . Ten o'clock? . . . Fine . . . See you then . . . Good night. (*He puts down the receiver.*) Ugh, what a silly business . . . and my mother's going to nag me the whole evening . . . what a profession . . . I dream of a day when there's no one left in the world but professional soldiers, then at last we'd have some peace and quiet . . . and no more wars . . . (*He calls out:*) Mama! . . . Mama! (*He leaves the room, still calling out.*)

CURTAIN

Act Two

Plantin's office. Behind the curtain, a conference room. In front of the curtain, a table, a chair and a telephone. Plantin's secretary, FRANCINE, *is seated at the table.* ROBERT, *Audubon's orderly, is sitting on the table, making lewd gestures at her behind his back.*

FRANCINE: You can say what you like but you'll never get me to hate Luis Mariano.

ROBERT: I don't care if you love him or hate him, all I'm saying is that he leaves me cold.

FRANCINE: Oh, but he sings so beautifully!

ROBERT: From words to action . . . (*He passes from words to action.*)

FRANCINE: Oh! Stop it immediately! Someone might come in!

ROBERT (*letting go of her*): Someone might not come in, and that's the whole beauty of it . . .

FRANCINE: You're always going above my head.

ROBERT: What about a little below the belt, then?

While he is embracing her, enter General KORKILOFF, *extremely Russian-looking.*

KORKILOFF (*coughing discreetly*): Excuse greatly, please. Tovarich Léon Plantin here, da?

FRANCINE: He'll be here any moment, sir; if you care to go into the conference room, he'll be with you right away . . . (*She shows him in and closes the door*

behind him. Lowering her voice.) He gives me the creeps that one.

ROBERT: That was General Korkiloff.

FRANCINE: He still gives me the creeps.

ROBERT (*dreamily*): What a handsome uniform . . .

FRANCINE: You'd look far better in it.

ROBERT: Hmm! Perhaps . . . (*About to clutch her as the doorbell rings again.*)

Enter General JACKSON.

JACKSON (*strong American accent*): Oops! Sorry to disturb you kids! Is Mr. Prime Minister Plantin here? He asked me to stop by.

FRANCINE: Why, yes, sir . . . I mean, General . . . please . . . this way. (*She shows him through to the conference room.*)

JACKSON: Well, thanks very much, young lady . . .

She closes the door on him, returns to her table and is just about to start doing some work when the same business occurs—doorbell sounds, enter General CHING PING TING, *and he is shown into the conference room. The curtain rises.*

CHING: Do you two know each other?

KORKILOFF: Gospodin Ching! Very greatly gratified to behold you.

JACKSON: Why, it's old Ching! Hell, what a surprise. And at Plantin's, of all places!

CHING (*to the other two*): My name is Ching Ping Ting, if you do not mind.

JACKSON: Aw, shucks. I'm awful sorry! . . .

KORKILOFF: A thousand apologies, tovarich . . .

CHING: I beg you humbly to excuse my unworthy mania for being addressed by full name. But what a surprise, indeed, to see you here, General Korkiloff! Ah, how well you look! And you, my dear Jackson, are positively glittering in your beautiful uniform. (*He shakes their hands in turn.*) Ah, do you know each other? Korkiloff, Jackson.

KORKILOFF *and* JACKSON *shake hands.*

KORKILOFF: Yes, believe we have most unfortunately already met at San Marino embassy.

JACKSON: Hey, wasn't it Andorra?

KORKILOFF: No longer remember, nitchevo, all embassies always full of Americans.

CHING: I am most happy that my most insignificant person has been present to effect introduction of two such great heroes.

KORKILOFF: Heroes! You exaggerate, comrade.

JACKSON: Yeah, I mean really, Ching, you'd hardly call Korkiloff a hero to look at him.

KORKILOFF: Oh, you possess tongue of serpent, very artful, is it issued to you under Marshall Plan?

JACKSON: Hey there, a little sense of humor, buddy.

KORKILOFF: Humor! May I remind you, humor was invented by engineer Boblitchkin in Moscow in 1713. Is scientifically proved.

CHING: Friends, friends, pray do not allow your tongues to entice you beyond your thoughts.

KORKILOFF: Ha! an American who *thinks*? . . .

CHING: Most regrettable, but yes. However, let us talk rather of what brings us all here. A message to my embassy requested own humble presence for urgent conference with honorable Prime Minister.

KORKILOFF: I also!

JACKSON: Yeah, me too!

CHING: A conference about what subject, do you think?

KORKILOFF: Hmm . . .

JACKSON: Yeah . . .

CHING: Yes . . . I see, of course, that we have reached the same conclusion. Do you gentlemen realize the complications which this project may involve?

KORKILOFF: With great preciseness. Da!

JACKSON: I sure do.

CHING: Well then, you are—as I believe they say in your country (*bowing to* JACKSON) —one up on me. I have no idea what Plantin wants of us.

KORKILOFF: Da, da! I was just about to say same thing!

JACKSON: I'll tell you what, Ching, you took the words right out of my mouth.

CHING: Of course, I am ill-equipped to guess what passes in the mind of mysterious occidental . . .

KORKILOFF: Besides, Franzouski never know what they want.

JACKSON: Yeah, and they don't have any bathrooms in their hotels.

KORKILOFF: And Russia invented automobile.

FRANCINE *escorts* AUDUBON *into the room.*

AUDUBON: Gentlemen . . .

Everyone bows ceremoniously.

Isn't Léon Plantin here yet?

CHING: We await him patiently.

AUDUBON: These damn civilians never have any sense of time.

KORKILOFF: Ah, you are so right. Da, da!

JACKSON: Well, gee, it's only just on the hour.

AUDUBON: No discipline.

JACKSON: Well, they're civilians, they don't need any discipline.

AUDUBON: Surely you are not trying to stick up for them, are you?

KORKILOFF: Typical American general: civilian in uniform.

AUDUBON: They don't have the advantage of the time-honored customs which set their mark on the magnificent products of our military training schools in Europe—St. Cyr . . .

JACKSON: St. Tropez.

CHING: Excuse, please . . . Very profound regrets, but we

too in Asia have been fighting for quite a long time now.

AUDUBON: Oh yes, indeed, indeed! . . . I had no intention of . . . And after all, you invented gunpowder!

KORKILOFF: Not true! Was orthodox pope Schwartzky during Middle Ages . . . first Stakhanovite in history.

JACKSON: O.K., O.K., the fact is the guy's late. Hey, Audubon, old boy, what's the score? Why did Plantin summon us?

CHING (*to* KORKILOFF): Practical outlook of Americans is best aspect of their character.

AUDUBON: Well . . . euh . . . military secrecy . . .

KORKILOFF: Ah, so, it is war, then? Here in Paris I am used to be summoned for so many trivial reasons . . . private views of art shows, mannequin parades, zakouski . . . Never know in advance . . .

AUDUBON: It does involve war up to a certain point, but that's merely incidental. The important thing is this —and listen, because I've been giving this problem a great deal of thought: don't you all think that, before it's too late, we should campaign for an international law which would stipulate that all generals accused of war crimes should be judged by other generals?

JACKSON: Listen, the German generals got off pretty easy at Nuremberg.

AUDUBON: Even so, the very idea of being judged by civilians is absolutely infuriating.

CHING: Your proposal seems to contain a certain measure of common interest.

AUDUBON: I hope I can count on the support of all of you, if the matter comes up . . .

PLANTIN *enters his secretary's office.*

PLANTIN: Hullo, my dear child . . . (*Obviously in a hurry.*) Is everything ready, Francine?

FRANCINE: The gentlemen are all waiting for you, Monsieur Plantin.

PLANTIN: What! Already! (*He looks at his watch.*) Yes, I must admit I am very late. Are they all there?

FRANCINE: Well, there's four of them, sir . . . All generals, in absolutely divine uniforms.

PLANTIN: In divine uniforms, eh? Is Audubon there?

FRANCINE: Yes, sir.

PLANTIN: Three generals and one degenerate, eh? Bring the secret minute-book with you and come along with me.

They both go in to join the generals.

So everybody's here! Good, good! Gentlemen, the French Republic salutes you. What will you have to drink?

FRANCINE *opens up the thick volume she has been carrying, to reveal inside it a well-stocked cocktail cabinet.*

Brandy, Pernod, Beaujolais? (*He rubs his hands together.*)

KORKILOFF
CHING   } (*together*): Beaujolais!
JACKSON

AUDUBON: I'll have a vodka-cola, please.

PLANTIN: Audubon, you'll drink Beaujolais like everybody else. (*To his secretary:*) One bottle and five glasses, please, Francine. (*He points to the vacant armchairs.*) Please be seated . . . Now, Audubon, would you be good enough to explain to these gentlemen the reason for our meeting?

AUDUBON: Listen, you know what it's all about, why don't *you* explain?

PLANTIN: Audubon, this is an order!

AUDUBON: You'll cover up for me?

PLANTIN: Yes, yes, I'll cover up for you.

AUDUBON: Sign a written statement.

PLANTIN: What written statement?

AUDUBON: Haven't you read *The Three Musketeers?*

PLANTIN: I can't rule the counry and read novels at the same time.

AUDUBON: Well, you're incapable of ruling the country, so you might as well read novels.

PLANTIN: Audubon, don't be cheeky. (*Speaking to the others:*) Please excuse us, gentlemen, Audubon doesn't know his ass from his elbow.

KORKILOFF: Don't mention it.

CHING: Carry on, please.

JACKSON: How about another drop of Beaujolais, huh? Only, this time, please, make mine a Holy Cow: that's half wine, half condensed milk.

FRANCINE *registers horrified surprise but scurries away to execute the order.*

AUDUBON: You read *The Three Musketeers*! Or, on second thought, don't. I'll dictate the statement to you. Francine, get ready to take something down . . . er, dictation. . . .

FRANCINE *picks up a sheet of paper and a pencil.*

"It is by my orders and for the good of the State that the undersigned has done what he has done: signed, Léon Plantin." Type that out in two copies.

PLANTIN: Is all that really in *The Three Musketeers*?

AUDUBON: Yes.

PLANTIN: Francine: make a note to order me a copy of that book. (*To* AUDUBON:) Is there a lot of stuff like that in *The Three Musketeers*?

AUDUBON: Oh, yes! All the way through.

PLANTIN: Incredible!

JACKSON: Yes indeed, a really great book.

PLANTIN: Ah, you have read it?

JACKSON: Sure! Well, as a comic, of course, with the words in those little balloons.

PLANTIN (*to* KORKILOFF *and* CHING): You too?

KORKILOFF *and* CHING (*together*): Certainly!

Meanwhile, FRANCINE *continues typing.*

KORKILOFF: Alexander Dumas grandmother Russian. I have read all his works.

PLANTIN: For goodness' sake, I'm the only one here who has never read him. No wonder the French always get the worst of it in diplomatic negotiations.

AUDUBON: Are you going to sign this document for me?

PLANTIN: I shall be proud to sign such an extraordinary text.

AUDUBON: Good. Now give me a glass of wine. If I get home drunk I can at least show this (*waving the sheet of paper*) to my mother.

PLANTIN: An excellent idea! (*Pours him a drink.*) Now, pray be good enough to explain to these gentlemen what is going on.

AUDUBON (*rising*): Gentlemen, it is war!

All rise.

KORKILOFF: Do you often find this mania for warmongering overcoming you?

CHING: I hope at least that you do not intend to fight all three of us?

AUDUBON (*sitting down again*): Gentlemen, please be seated, you did not quite understand what I was saying.

PLANTIN: But you're talking tripe, you silly prick! How do you expect them to understand?

AUDUBON: Oh, explain it yourself, then!

PLANTIN: Listen, Wilson, you are absolutely impossible. Next time, I'm going to hand over the command to Dupont.

AUDUBON: What! That rotten old queen!

PLANTIN: Well, try to explain matters properly!

AUDUBON: Hmm! The truth is, gentlemen, that basically our problems stem from the fact that . . . euh . . . the present economic situation is . . . euh . . . complicated . . . indeed, one may even say, critical. To sum up: Work, Family, Nation, as it used to say on the coins! Three cheers for the Unknown Soldier! All honor to the martyrs of the Resistance! Everyone united behind the tricolor! (*He rises again.*) Gentlemen, it is war.

PLANTIN: Audubon, you really are a stupid bugger.

AUDUBON: Well, I'm a soldier; you shouldn't expect me to be able to explain all this political claptrap.

PLANTIN: Oh, all right . . . Sit down, everybody. I will explain. Now gentlemen, the fact is that in France our industrialists and agricultural producers find themselves in the unfortunate position of having to go to war in order to absorb a totally unexpected and extremely regrettable overproduction pattern. I have therefore ordered General Wilson de la Pétardière, here, the commander of my G.H.Q., to take all necessary measures. And the bloody fool has been farting around without even troubling to find out who the hell we are supposed to be fighting. Which is why I have taken the liberty of asking you to attend this meeting: I ask you one question frankly, gentlemen —would any of you like to take us on?

KORKILOFF: Niet! Have other possibilities in mind.

CHING: Ah no! Regret we have prior engagements, as you know.

JACKSON (*pointing at* CHING): Yeah . . . as far as that goes, I agree with him.

PLANTIN: Gentlemen, France has played second fiddle for too long now in international politics. I am sure you will understand that the glorious history of our country does not permit us to wait while you make up your minds. I must insist that France should remain at the head of civilization and retain the initiative in this field, as we do already in the fields of cookery, dressmaking, champagne production and perfume making. So I repeat: which of you wants to take us on?

AUDUBON: Some more wine, Francine.

FRANCINE *pours him a drink.*

CHING: Ah sorry, not interested.

JACKSON: You can count us out, that's for sure.

KORKILOFF: Niet! Impossible to oblige you. You too small for mighty Soviet Union. Choose someone your own size.

PLANTIN: Come now, a little cooperation, please, gentlemen!

KORKILOFF: Can you not find some country like . . . well . . . Venezuela? . . . or Tierra del Fuego? . . .

AUDUBON (*indignantly*): Really, sir! You might just as well suggest the Principality of Monaco! What about our national prestige! Our *gloire*!

CHING: Why not England?

PLANTIN: Hmm! Unfortunately, that country has insisted for several years now on a policy of friendship which makes it difficult for us to attack them without prior collusion.

AUDUBON: Couldn't we evoke the memory of Joan of Arc? Or Waterloo?

PLANTIN: Waterloo? Pfff . . . Why not Fashoda or Mers-el-Kebir, then? No, no. England's out of the question. Apart from anything else, we'd have every hotel manager along the Riviera screaming at us.

KORKILOFF: Italy?

PLANTIN: Come now! It takes two to make a fight.

JACKSON: Listen, you can deal us out in any case. Our boys have enough to do around the world without coming back to France again. Oh no! Once bitten, twice shy! You made suckers out of us in 1944, remember? What a load of chizzlers, you French.

PLANTIN: Damn and blast! So nobody wants a war?

CHING: Nobody? Excuse me, honorable Plantin, if I laugh. What about Africa?

PLANTIN: Well, what about Africa?

CHING: Declare war on Morocco or Algeria! Your country possesses such a glorious past, such vast ex-colonies, I am sure you can wage magnificent war on them. And think of enormous territory involved.

PLANTIN (*looking at* AUDUBON): My God, he's right!

AUDUBON: He's right.

PLANTIN: Splendid solution!

AUDUBON: Splendid.

CHING: And please allow me to offer you one modest suggestion in addition? . . .

AUDUBON: Oh, please do, Ching!

CHING (*bowing*): Ching Ping Ting, if it is not too much to ask.

PLANTIN: Speak your mind, Ching Ping Ting Ling Ding!

CHING: Well, gentlemen, if you decide to wage war in Africa, my very humble nation will esteem it a privilege to join in the invasion. . . . We will send you one division of Volunteer Freedom Fighters.

KORKILOFF: We also! Two divisions!

JACKSON: A grand idea! Now, I'm just thinking. . . . We could send a whole contingent of Negro troops! Why stop just at Algeria and Morocco? . . . The whole of Africa, huh? That would automatically solve the whole color problem. . . . We'll send you our own blacks, who will wipe out your African blacks and vice versa . . . and if there are any survivors . . . well . . .

PLANTIN: That sounds a very promising solution.

AUDUBON: Yes! Yes! (*Working himself up into a frenzy of enthusiasm.*) Battles! Carnage! War! The infantry! Ping! ping! I mean, bang, bang! Ah! . . . A glass of wine, please, Francine.

PLANTIN (*rising*): Gentlemen! In the name of the government of our Republic, I have the honor to thank you for the invaluable contribution you have just made toward the solution of a problem of extreme national interest. General Ching Ping Ting, it will be a great personal pleasure for me to award you the Grand Cross of the Legion of Honor.

CHING: Have had that great honor five times already, thank

you . . . but please . . . most happy to accept yet again . . .

PLANTIN: Francine! . . . Bring a type-three declaration of war. We must get this all down in black and white. . . . Ho, ho. Purely typographical, of course!

AUDUBON (*delighted by this witticism*): Oh, you are a devil!

FRANCINE (*collapsing exhausted*): Yes, Monsieur Plantin.

KORKILOFF (*very amiably to* JACKSON): Now at last we will have a chance to see your latest model tank.

JACKSON: Yeah . . . It should come in very handy. Now you'll be able to try out your new rapid-fire anti-tank gun on it. My congratulations, Ching: a great idea. A little propaganda and the whole thing will get off to a swinging start.

KORKILOFF: Hmm! Propaganda. Da. Certainly. But on what, may I ask, will you base your own propaganda?

JACKSON: Oh, it's a sure-fire slogan, guaranteed by the Army Medical Corps. (*He declaims.*) "Nowadays the wounded never die."

KORKILOFF: That may be all right for your civilians, but in Russia it would not work. In our country, impossible to imagine the military offering to heal citizen's wounds.

CHING: And please, allow me to observe very humbly that it is proved scientifically that to repair a soldier on the field of battle turns him into a disabled serviceman who must be awarded special pension, which is very expensive. Also disabled serviceman is not pleasant to behold, so constitutes bad propaganda. I agree with the profound observation of my esteemed friend Korkiloff that it would be preferable to encourage the progress of civilian medical technique. A repaired civilian is always eager to become a soldier, to prove that he is fit. Always so in China.

PLANTIN: Look, these are mere details. Are we agreed on the essential points?

KORKILOFF: Da!

JACKSON: O.K. by me, pal!

CHING: Yes. Agree, honorable Plantin.

PLANTIN: Good, then we'll sign a little treaty, shall we? Francine! (*She appears.*) Darling . . . bring me all that stuff I asked you to get ready . . . you know what . . .

FRANCINE: Immediately, sir.

AUDUBON: What! . . . You have predicted the way matters would turn out with such precision? Ah! Plantin, that's strong, that's really very strong! (*To the others:*) He is very strong! We are very strong! And this is very strong! (*He lifts his glass.*) Gentlemen, I give you the toast! To the empire builders, to those who are about to die, to the happy outcome of the present enterprise, and to little Francine's beauty spot.

All rise and clink glasses.

Gentlemen, I have the pleasure to inform you that Plantin is going to treat us all to lunch at Maxim's.

PLANTIN (*hisses at* AUDUBON): What on earth are you talking about? Are you trying to ruin me?

AUDUBON (*hisses back at* PLANTIN): Increase the Defense Estimates! (*Rises.*) Right! Attention, everyone in line!

They march off in Indian file. AUDUBON *brings up the rear, singing a little jingle*:

> Oh, Maxim, here we come,
> Better oil your maxim-gun,
> Our maxim is to have fun,
> And now we're going to grab some.
> Oh, Maxim, here we come,
> We've got them on the run,
> And we'll drown their dying screams
> With frolics at Maxim's.

CURTAIN

Act Three

A front-line underground command post, occupied by a front line consisting of Generals AUDUBON, LAVESTE, JUILLET *and* DUPONT D'ISIGNY. *One wall of the room carries a chart of military operations which is in fact a map of the Tour de France bicycle race, which, as a result of a general retreat, has been temporarily transferred to Sweden. In other words, it is a map of Sweden. When the curtain rises, four camp beds can be seen in a row. Three of these are occupied by* DUPONT, LAVESTE *and* JUILLET. AUDUBON, *awake and fully dressed, is striding furiously to and fro in the confined space, a space rendered even more confined by the presence of a table and various necessary props, and the fact that, in any case, this whole play is being acted on a tiny stage, since no respectable company would dream of performing it.*

AUDUBON (*talking to himself*): Disgraceful . . . Just look at them lying there! Not a care in the world! What a collection! (*Laughs derisively.*) And they call themselves soldiers! (*He paces around and around like a wild beast, although it must be admitted that a wild beast would be more likely to pace up and down if its cage was quadrilateral.*) All of them—sleeping like logs!

JUILLET *opens one eye and raises himself on his elbows.*

JUILLET (*sleepily*): That's funny. You say "like a log" whereas I . . . I . . . I say "like a dog." (*He falls back onto his bed, with a loud snore.*)

AUDUBON: What? (*Shrugs his shoulders.*) Logs. Of course that's the right word.

DUPONT (*same business as* JUILLET): I . . . I say "like hogs."

DUPONT *collapses.* AUDUBON *turns toward* LAVESTE.

AUDUBON (*angrily*): Go on! You too! You may as well have your say on the subject. What is your favorite phrase, may I ask? Like logs, dogs or hogs? Like fatheads, perhaps, or numskulls? (*Getting increasingly annoyed.*) Dumbbells, huh? Or Vichy politicians? (*He stamps his feet with rage.*) Like the blessed saints? They are sleeping like the saints? God, today's crop of generals makes one sick! (*He hurls some object to the floor, a book or a bronze vase.*) Maybe that will wake you up! (*No movement from the others.*) No? Try *that,* then! (*He picks up a large clock and hurls it to the floor where it smashes with a loud jangling of broken mechanism. He looks at the recumbent generals.*) Still no effect! Ah, it seems hopeless . . . (*He seizes a bugle and blows into it, but no sound emerges and he hurls it aside.*) Lousy rotten useless instrument! (*Exhausted, he collapses into a chair at the table.*) Oh, I'm so tired . . . (*He gets up again, goes and sits on the side of his bed, yawns.*) Aaaaah! (*He lies down.*) Time for beddy-byes, Audubon . . .

At exactly that moment, with clockwork precision and identical movements, the three others, fully dressed, sit up in their beds, swivel around, plant their feet on the ground, then stand up and clap their kepis on their heads in the same motion. All three stand in line by Audubon's bed.

JUILLET: What's this, Wilson? Not awake yet?

AUDUBON (*drowsily*): What? (*He sits up.*) Oh, my God, it's you.

DUPONT: Certainly it's us. . . . What about us?

AUDUBON: Oh, leave me alone.

JUILLET: How do you mean, alone? (*Brandishing a teddy bear which he has found under Audubon's pillow.*)

AUDUBON: Alone, I tell you!

DUPONT: But what on earth's eating you?

JUILLET: Come now, you can see that poor old Wilson is feeling seedy. What's the matter, old man?

AUDUBON (*sulkily*): Nothing.

JUILLET: We're all pals here . . . you can tell us . . .

AUDUBON: What a rotten sleep I've just had.

JUILLET: Well, I think our little mess is pretty comfy.

AUDUBON: It may seem funny to you, but I just can't get to sleep unless my mother has tucked me in first.

DUPONT (*exasperated*): Oh!

JUILLET: Calm down, Dupont . . .

DUPONT: He slays me, he and his mother . . .

LAVESTE: What did you say?

DUPONT: I said he slays me.

LAVESTE: That's just what I thought I heard you say. (*He shakes a large money box under Dupont's nose.*) Pay a fine, please!

JUILLET: You should know that there are some words which we simply don't mention in this establishment.

DUPONT (*shrugs his shoulders and pays*): I prefer not to comment!

AUDUBON: Well, I certainly intend to comment! When you were sniveling yesterday morning because you hadn't heard from your little plumber's mate, I didn't say anything . . . If anyone in this room is ridiculous it's you!

DUPONT: Wilson, your position of command does not authorize you to be indiscreet!

AUDUBON: What a slob! Huh! To think that one is obliged to associate with perverts like him!

JUILLET: Gentlemen, please!

LAVESTE: I agree with Juillet. If, in the present state of enforced inactivity in which we find ourselves, we allow our little discussions to take on a sour note, only regrettable consequences can ensue.

JUILLET (*aside*): But I didn't say that . . . Pity . . . rather good, wish I had.

DUPONT: What's all this about inactivity? What are you insinuating now? That I'm not waging war with the utmost vigor?

LAVESTE: Look, Dupont . . . d'Isigny . . . I'm speaking for all four of us. You know perfectly well what I mean.

AUDUBON: There's no doubt about it, the front is stagnant.

DUPONT (*drily*): At a hundred feet underground, that's hardly surprising.

AUDUBON: Listen, you're getting more and more unbearable. The others opposite are a hundred feet underground too, aren't they?

JUILLET: Be reasonable, Dupont. We are no longer living in the times of bayonet charges! Our most important objective in these days is to ensure that our troops' commanders are preserved intact to provide leadership.

DUPONT: Yes, and meanwhile all the fighting is going on in the rear. (*He is almost dancing with rage.*) Oh, it's so infuriating!

AUDUBON (*winking at the others*): I know how to calm him down. Dupont . . .

DUPONT: If you forget just once again to address me by my full name, I shall not speak a word to you for three days.

AUDUBON: What a firebrand. Listen. This is what I suggest. Do you remember, about two years ago? When we all had a little party at my place?

JUILLET (*with a note of distaste in his voice*): Hmm, yes . . .

The other two answer in a similar fashion.

AUDUBON: Well, we'll organize a little party just between ourselves—like before.

DUPONT: Oh, no, thanks! Not again! It would bore us all to death!

LAVESTE: I beg your pardon?

DUPONT: To death, I said. I want nothing to do with it!

JUILLET: Pay a fine, please (*He rattles the box at* DUPONT, *who grumbles but puts money in.*)

DUPONT: I don't mind paying a fine but the very idea of another of his tea parties makes me feel quite sick.

AUDUBON: What a rotten friend you are!

DUPONT: You've seen what your first tea party led to! One experience like that is quite enough for me!

AUDUBON (*annoyed*): All right . . . All right . . . I won't insist, I won't insist. Since you're being so beastly about my idea, think up something yourself! I'm simply not going to bother about you any more! Find your own amusement! Go on, go on!

DUPONT: There are exactly thirty-six other ways in which four people can enjoy themselves together.

JUILLET: Dupont, your personal moral values in no way oblige you to propose obscene projects to us . . .

DUPONT: Don't be ridiculous. In the first place, had I wanted to propose obscene projects I would have said thirty-two ways. And in the second place, none of you stand a hope in hell—you're all far too ugly!

LAVESTE: As opposed to your pretty little plumber's mate!

AUDUBON (*rubs his hands and says sarcastically*): I see that your suggestion is no more successful than mine!

DUPONT: You're a bunch of pigs!

JUILLET: Listen, everyone, why don't we play a game?

LAVESTE: Ah! At last, a good idea!

AUDUBON: A good idea? Hmm. It depends on what game.

LAVESTE: Oh, I know an amusing game. I remember we used to play it all the time at home. My father taught

us how to play it. I'm sure you'll like it. It's called
Pumping the Organ.

JUILLET: Splendid!

AUDUBON: It certainly sounds intriguing!

LAVESTE: I'm sure it will amuse you. Right, all take your
places.

JUILLET: Where? What do we do?

LAVESTE: Well, it's rather like playing pinochle, if I remember rightly . . . Four around a table.

JUILLET: Well, you're wrong then, because in that case it
must be like bridge . . .

AUDUBON: Oh, nonsense! I'm sure we all walk around the
table, like in Musical Chairs.

DUPONT (*impatiently*): Nothing of the sort. It's two teams,
like in Prisoner's Base!

JUILLET (*rising and holding out the money box*): You certainly have money to spare, my dear friend. Come on,
another twenty in the box, please.

DUPONT: Oh damn! (*He pays up, then goes and sits down.*)

JUILLET: That's the spirit, old man. . . . Pay up without any
fuss. No petty squabbles here.

AUDUBON: You're absolutely right—no petty squabbles. Dupont-d'Isigny, I propose a handshake all round.

DUPONT (*mechanically*): I repeat that my full name is . . .
(*Comes to himself.*) Hmm, yes, you're quite right.
Sorry! Sorry! Sorry! (*He shakes hands with the other
three in turn.*)

JUILLET: How does one play?

Everybody sits at the table.

LAVESTE: One sec, old boy, I'm just trying to remember . . . Let's see now . . . Ah yes, first we have to choose a prickateer . . .

AUDUBON: Ooooh! Let *me* be the prickateer!

LAVESTE: Well, I have no objection, if it's all right with the rest of you. Yes? Go on, then. As prickateer you have to take twenty packs of cards, shuffle together carefully and deal 233 cards to each player . . . one by one . . . reversing the direction of distribution every sixth round . . . no, every seventh round . . . oh, bother . . .

AUDUBON (*alarmed*): Would anyone like to swap being prickateer?

DUPONT: No, thanks.

JUILLET: No, you wanted to be *it* yourself.

LAVESTE: Now, let me think for a moment. (*Mumbles to himself.*) If a red deuce follows a black four . . . the prickateer deals seventeen cards to the player immediately preceding the one who has taken two consecutive tricks . . . euh . . . no . . . three consecutive tricks . . . on condition that at least one of those tricks contains a red ace. . . . Ah yes, now I'm beginning to remember. . . . To begin with, one has to decide who is going to play first. For that we need a jostler.— Who wants to be the jostler?

AUDUBON: Me! me!

LAVESTE: No, you're already the prickateer.— Dupont?

DUPONT: No, thanks.

LAVESTE: How about you, Juillet?

JUILLET: No, I'm not being jostler.

LAVESTE: Well, it will have to be me, then. Good. Each player begins by giving five hundred francs to the jostler to pay him for his services.

AUDUBON: Hey, how about the prickateer?

LAVESTE: Ah no, it's not the same thing. You volunteered for the job: if you hadn't done so, we'd have had to draw lots. Whereas the jostler is always co-opted. One of the fascinating things about this game is how absolutely unfair it is.

AUDUBON (*groans*): Five hundred francs . . . Hmm! It's lucky we are all on active duty pay, otherwise . . .

The three pay up.

JUILLET: Tell us the rest, Laveste, this is beginning to sound really exciting.

LAVESTE: Let's not rush at it, please, it's all rather complicated.

AUDUBON: And you call the game Pumping the Organ!

LAVESTE: Yes . . . at least, that's what it was known as in my family. Now then, let's see. . . . The jostler starts by quitting the game and circling the table three times while holding his nose. (*He executes this maneuver, then comes to an abrupt halt.*) But, I say: have we got twenty packs of cards?

JUILLET: Have we, Audubon?

AUDUBON: I'm sure we haven't. In any case, mama has always forbidden me to play cards.

DUPONT: I can't stand card games.

LAVESTE: Well, then, there's not much point in my going on, is there? Besides, I've forgotten the rules.

AUDUBON (*sighs with relief*): Huh! What a relief!

LAVESTE (*brightly*): But if you feel like it, there's another game we could play, called Bashing the Bishop.

JUILLET: Hmm! . . .

DUPONT: Yes . . .

AUDUBON: That doesn't sound quite so promising as Pumping the Organ.

LAVESTE: Of course I don't recall all the rules of that game either, but I do remember that it was good fun.

Silence. All drum their fingers on the table increasingly loudly. Suddenly the door opens and ROBERT *enters, in full military gear, carrying a folded newspaper.*

ROBERT: *Figaro! Figaro!*

AUDUBON: Ah!

They all rush at ROBERT *to seize the paper, but* AUDUBON *restrains them with an imperious gesture.*

Allow me, gentlemen. Thank you, Robert!

ROBERT: Don't mention it, sir.

AUDUBON: You may dismiss.

ROBERT *leaves the room.*

DUPONT: What's the news? Come on!

LAVESTE: Come on, read it to us!

JUILLET: Yes, what's going on?

AUDUBON slowly and carefully unfolds the newspaper: it turns out to be Le Figaro, *completely blank, entirely censored throughout, apart from the title.*

AUDUBON: You can see for yourselves! (*He turns the pages.*)

DUPONT: Well, that's splendid! At least the censors are on the march.

JUILLET: They must be the only ones who are!

They all look at LAVESTE.

AUDUBON: Laveste . . . do you not think that the departments under your command seem to be perhaps a trifle . . . euh . . . punctilious?

LAVESTE: Hmm! You know . . . one can't tell the public everything . . . There are certain items of news which, if published, might arouse alarm and despondency . . .

AUDUBON (*gesturing at the newspaper*): But all the same, don't you think . . .

LAVESTE: Oh no, not at all. No news is good news!

JUILLET: How right you are!

AUDUBON: Yes indeed!

LAVESTE: Besides, this newspaper in its present form is entirely suitable for being reissued as the next edition. . . . An enormous saving! And as you see, we can go on offering the public sixteen-page newspapers.

AUDUBON counts the pages.

AUDUBON: He's right! Sixteen pages!

LAVESTE: Very important psychologically.

AUDUBON: I'm sure you're right.

> DUPONT *buries his head in the newspaper. Silence. Same business as at the end of the previous scene: fingers drumming increasingly loudly on the table, then suddenly stopping.*

> But still, can anyone tell me why we don't seem to be able to re-create the old atmosphere of camaraderie?

JUILLET: You are asking us?

AUDUBON: Indeed I am. With sorrow and amazement.

JUILLET: Because there's a war on. Didn't you know?

> DUPONT *rises and thrusts the money box at* JUILLET, *who duly pays his fine.*

AUDUBON: But, of course, how silly of me!—It's all Plantin's fault. My mother warned me that he was bad company for me to keep.

> *The sound of a gun being fired.*

> What's that? But what's going on? Oh, my God, it sounds like a . . .

JUILLET (*worried*): It certainly did seem to be . . .

DUPONT (*delighted*): Ah! At last!

LAVESTE: What do you mean, at last? You must be out of your mind. Don't you think we have enough trouble as it is?

> ROBERT *reappears.*

ROBERT: Sir . . .There are visitors.

AUDUBON: Visitors, what visitors? But before anything else, tell me what was that noise we heard just now?

ROBERT: Sir, the fort commander thought it might be appropriate to fire a salvo in honor of the visitors. . . . Euh, the guns were beginning to get rusty, so he thought that firing a few rounds would cheer up the men and exercise the equipment . . .

AUDUBON (*furious*): You can go and tell him that it was a damn stupid idea. A complete waste of manpower and material. Make it quite clear to him that I never want to hear that particular sound again. In any case, it's quite fantastic: who's supposed to be in command around here? It's going to cost him a fine of fifty francs for our fine box!

ROBERT: I'll get it from him, General de la Pétardière, sir.

AUDUBON: Now, who are these visitors?

ROBERT: The Prime Minister, sir, accompanied by General Korkiloff, Monseigneur Tapecul and General Ching.

AUDUBON: And Jackson?

ROBERT: I didn't see him, sir.

AUDUBON: What a mess! It's a madhouse!

ROBERT *is about to leave.*

One moment. (*He goes up to the wall map.*)

Who won today's stage of the race?

ROBERT: Robic, sir, with Bartali second.

AUDUBON: Well, what the hell happened to Koblet? He's

petering out like he did two years ago. Darn! (*He alters the positions of the little flags sticking in the map.*)

JUILLET: I'm afraid Biquet is going to lose ground on the Stockholm-Malmö stage.

AUDUBON: Nonsense, Juillet, he could win in a wheelchair.

LAVESTE: Speaking for myself, I can't make head or tail of the Tour de France since it moved to Sweden. At least we had recognizable landmarks before, like the Galibier and Izoard mountain passes. Now the whole thing is completely incomprehensible.

DUPONT (*sarcastically*): But no more complicated, surely, than your famous card games, Laveste . . .

JUILLET: I suppose we should be grateful that the Swedes agreed to take over the race. Suppose it had been transferred to Azerbaijan . . .

ROBERT: Excuse me, gentlemen . . . (*To* AUDUBON:) Sir, shall I show them in?

AUDUBON: Yes, yes, right away. Wait, though: do you have anything for us to drink?

ROBERT: Oh no, sir. And I'm completely broke.

AUDUBON (*turning to the other generals*): Why, of course! (*Holding out his hand.*) Laveste . . . since you are no longer the jostler . . . (*To* DUPONT *and* JUILLET:) I'm sure you too will be glad to contribute your share to the purchase of some stimulating potion . . .

DUPONT: No anisette, huh!

JUILLET: Come on, cough up that 1500 francs.

LAVESTE (*to* AUDUBON): Oh, all right.

AUDUBON (*to* ROBERT): Euh . . . buy a bottle of port. A thousand francs will be enough.

ROBERT (*leaving*): Yes, sir.

AUDUBON: Splendid! (*He pockets the rest of the money.*) Run off to the canteen then. Bring a few cakes, too. (*He rubs his hands together.*) We'll be able to have our little tea party after all.

DUPONT: I must say, you are the most horribly civilian general I have ever met.

AUDUBON (*fussing around*): Let's get everything ready! A little tablecloth . . . doesn't anyone have a little table-cloth?

DUPONT (*exasperated*): What on earth would we be carry-ing little tablecloths around with us for?

AUDUBON: At home, mama has lots and lots of little table-cloths stowed away in all the cupboards. So con-venient. (*He runs around, opening drawers.*) Now, let's see. What could we possibly use as a little table-cloth? (*To* JUILLET:) Ah, Juillet! Do you still have that white flag you used to carry around with you?

JUILLET: I suppose so.

AUDUBON: Can I borrow it, please?

JUILLET: You really are a nuisance. It will get covered in stains.

AUDUBON: Are you refusing?

JUILLET: Am I to consider that as an ultimatum?

AUDUBON: Juillet, give me your white flag. It's not an ultimatum, it's an order.

JUILLET: If it's an order, that's different. (*He goes to look for his white flag.*)

AUDUBON: Flowers . . . we must have flowers. Nothing brightens up a day like a pretty bouquet of posies.

LAVESTE (*meditatively*): Perhaps one of them might remember the rules of Pumping the Organ better than I can?

DUPONT: I hope not!

AUDUBON: And what can we do about decorations? Dupont, do you happen to have any little Christmas lights with you?

DUPONT: For Christ's sake! What in blazes do you think I'd be doing on front-line duty festooned with strings of Christmas lights?

AUDUBON: Well, we always had them at home. Every Christmas, my mama used to arrange them around the dining-room chandelier and turn them on.

DUPONT (*enraged*): Ah, this is too much! Are you going to go on for ever boring the balls off us with cretinous reminiscences of your bed-wetting childhood? I swear to you, it's enough to drive one to suicide!

JUILLET: Hmm! The fine box, old man . . . (*He passes him the box.*)

DUPONT (*furious*): Oh, piss off. (*He strides toward the door and bumps into* ROBERT *who has just entered and is standing on one side to let the small group of visitors pass.*)

Enter PLANTIN, KORKILOFF *and* CHING.

PLANTIN: Ah, there they are. (*To his companions*:) I knew we'd find them somewhere. (*Embracing* AUDUBON.) Wilson! My dear friend. What a pleasure to find you all still alive!

AUDUBON: Oh! Plantin . . . I'm in an absolute tizzy . . . nothing's ready. . . . We simply weren't expecting you, you see! Poor you, to come all this way and then be faced by this utter shambles!

PLANTIN: Don't worry, old man—the pleasure of seeing you again is more than ample recompense!

AUDUBON: Dear oh dear, I'm quite confused. . . . (*He greets the other visitors.*) My dear General Korkiloff . . . and you, Ching Ping Ting . . . Allow me to present my General Staff . . . Dupont-d'Isigny, Lenvers de Laveste, Juillet . . .

Hand shakes, polite exclamations, etc., all around, then ROLAND TAPECUL *enters, carrying a bottle.*

ROLAND: I've just discovered your crummy orderly in the act of sampling the contents of this bottle. It beats me why you still allow that creep to hang around. . . . This is all that's left.

Enter ROBERT, *carrying two plates of dry cakes.*

AUDUBON: Robert! What happened to the port?

ROBERT (*to* ROLAND): Shall I tell him the truth, Monseigneur?

ROLAND: Shut up, you chowderhead. I have pronounced *my* version of the incident . . . It's as good as dogma now.

ROBERT (*aside*): A load of papal bull.

ROLAND slips him a banknote. ROBERT *sets the cakes on the table and leaves the room.* ROLAND, KORKILOFF *and* CHING *begin discreetly nibbling their snack.*

PLANTIN: My dear Wilson, we are pressed for time so I shall be brief and to the point. We are at the moment making a tour of inspection of the front line, so of course we have included your command post in our itinerary. Everything is going well.

AUDUBON: Oh, good.

PLANTIN: But surely you are in touch with the situation?

AUDUBON: Well . . . euh . . . you know, the news in the papers is rather vague, and we lead a very quiet life here. In my view it's impossible to get any work done in a command post if everyone's rushing around all the time. So we take it very easy.

PLANTIN (*pointing to the map*): Ah! The good old Tour de France!

They all nod and sigh nostalgically.

DUPONT: Mr. Prime Minister, to be quite frank with you I can tell you that I personally am bored stiff.

PLANTIN: Ah, you too? So am I, I must say.

LAVESTE: What remedy do you adopt?

PLANTIN: Well, as you see, tours of inspection. Moscow one day, Washington the next. The company of these gentlemen is extremely diverting, I must admit. (*Gesturing toward the three apostles who are busy stuffing their mouths with cake.*)

AUDUBON: Here today, gone tomorrow . . .

PLANTIN: As I have just said, the news is excellent. The French economy is at last completely unbalanced.

JUILLET *and* LAVESTE: Aah!

AUDUBON: Hmm! Is that such a good thing?

PLANTIN: Of course! Now is the time when we politicians can show what stuff we are made of. Here's how I see it: you people bring the war to a close as speedily as possible—by a victory, of course—and we shall re-establish the situation.

> JUILLET *goes up to* PLANTIN *with the money box in his hand and rattles it at him.* PLANTIN *makes a gesture of puzzled astonishment.*

PLANTIN: What on earth's that?

JUILLET: It's our little money box for paying fines. There are certain forbidden words . . .

PLANTIN: Which ones?

JUILLET: Obviously, I can't tell you, otherwise I'd be letting myself in for a fine. But don't worry, we'll let you know what they are as soon as you say them.

AUDUBON: Come, come, now. (*To* PLANTIN:) Yes . . . I see . . . I understand your point of view. But, of course, as soon as the . . . hmm . . . the thing is over, you will be cutting down on the estimates for . . . hmm . . . *our* estimates?

> *During this speech, business by* JUILLET *who keeps getting the fine box ready to present, but is frustrated each time.*

PLANTIN: That goes without saying.

AUDUBON: Hmm! And you want a victory?

PLANTIN: What a question!

AUDUBON: Listen . . . I'm sorry, but I'm afraid that that's not very feasible at the moment . . .

PLANTIN: What! Listen, Wilson, you must be out of your mind! I'm not asking you, I'm telling you.

AUDUBON: It's an order? You'll cover up for me?

PLANTIN: Haven't I always done so?

AUDUBON: All right, then! (*To the others:*) My friends, you may consider the . . . the job is now over.

JUILLET *holds out the box during this speech but is disappointed again.*

DUPONT (*furiously*): Oh no! Not already! Damn!

AUDUBON: Well, almost over . . . after the next victory.

DUPONT: Ah, that's a bit better. We don't have to hoof it tomorrow, then?

AUDUBON: My dear d'Isigny . . . I intend, in fact, to assign the operation in question to you . . .

DUPONT: I accept! May I go and get ready?

AUDUBON: Go on, off with you, then! What a big baby!

DUPONT: Ha! (*He salutes and marches off.*)

PLANTIN: The morale of your subordinates is astonishing!

AUDUBON: Yes . . . euh . . . I have them all well in hand.

PLANTIN: I'm counting on you!

AUDUBON: I won't let you down!

PLANTIN: Let's drink a toast to that, shall we?

AUDUBON: Yes, a drink . . . if those three greedy hogs haven't guzzled it all.

They go and join the others at the table.

Robert!

ROBERT *appears.*

ROBERT: Sir!

AUDUBON: More booze!

ROBERT *rubs the tips of his thumb and index finger together.*

Money, always money! Damn! Ask Plantin! Or no, ask Roland.

ROLAND (*rises*): What? What is he to ask me?

AUDUBON: For some of the necessary . . .

ROLAND (*bursts out laughing*): Some of the necessary! Really, you old fossil, your slang is as out of date as a paternoster. (*Brings some money out of his pocket.*) Here's some loot, buddy!

ROBERT (*annoyed*): Hmm, I always call it lolly.

ROLAND: Yes, but you don't have any responsibilities. Hop to it now!

ROBERT *hurries off, returns with bottles, then goes out again.*

AUDUBON (*emotionally*): You're still as malicious as ever,

but it's nice to see you again all the same, you **son-of-a-bitch.**

ROLAND: Come on, squeeze out a tear or two!

AUDUBON: Oh, you infuriate me!

ROLAND (*slaps him on the shoulder*): A drink.

They join the group.

LAVESTE: We were getting so bored, you know, that I even tried to teach them a card game, Pumping the Organ . . .

Loud laughter all around.

. . . but they couldn't get the hang of it.

PLANTIN: My poor friends. Fortunately, this . . . all this will soon be over!

JUILLET *had seized the fine box and now puts it down again.*

JUILLET (*annoyed*): I must say, you learn fast!

KORKILOFF: Ah, is terrible, strategic boredom, Russia invented it.

CHING: Not so. Known in China since Ting dynasty.

AUDUBON: Tang!

CHING: Ah, tang you!

AUDUBON: Well, what I like best of all is a nice party game with a few good pals.

KORKILOFF (*to* LAVESTE): Russian folklore very rich in social games!

LAVESTE (*interested*): Oh, really?

ROLAND: Listen, my children, how about us all singing a song?

AUDUBON: Oh yes, a marvelous idea! (*To* JUILLET:) No, Juillet, for once you're going to put away your old money-box and we'll all sing a marching song!

ROLAND (*disappointed*): Oh . . . no! (*Brightening.*) Well, some really disgusting student song, then. What was that one I learned at the seminary? . . . (*Thinks.*)

KORKILOFF (*to* LAVESTE *again*): Da, many social games . . . Please, do you know Russian Roulette? (*He shows him a six-shooter and extracts the bullets from the cylinder.*)

AUDUBON: I'll start off, chaps . . . (*He coughs and scratches his throat.*)

KORKILOFF: You leave one bullet in gun . . . then make cylinder spin, so . . . like in bingo . . .

LAVESTE: Bingo Bango Bongo, I don't want to leave the Congo . . .

KORKILOFF: Very droll. Quiet, please, I explain game— spin cylinder—press trigger, so. (*He puts the revolver to his forehead and pulls the trigger. Nothing happens. He bursts out laughing.*) Ha ha!

LAVESTE: Ah . . . oh well . . .

KORKILOFF: Try!

Offers him the revolver. LAVESTE *is scared to death but takes it. During this business,* AUDUBON *starts off on his song.*

AUDUBON:

March on

March on
March on, march on, march on
Let's march with pace so keen
Along a road that's green
March on
March on.

Applause.

Let's imitate the sound of marching feet!

ALL (*together*): Plonk! Plonk! Plonk! Plonk! Plonk! Plonk! Plonk!

ROLAND: My turn!

He coughs and scratches his throat, while LAVESTE, *having at last plucked up his courage, pulls the trigger of the revolver on himself, without result. Relieved, he roars with laughter, joined by* KORKILOFF.

A little quiet, please!

March on
March on
March on, march on, march on
Let's march all upside down
Along a road that's brown
March on
March on.

The others repeat the same refrain of marching feet. LAVESTE *has passed the revolver to* CHING PING TING, *who slaps his thigh, takes the revolver and asks* LAVESTE *and* KORKILOFF *in a low voice for instructions.*

JUILLET: Me! Me now! I've got a good one!

> March on
> March on
> March on, march on, march on
> Let's march with step that's slack
> Along a road that's black
> March on
> March on.

AUDUBON: Ah! Juillet! You're ripe for election to the Académie!

General enthusiasm. CHING *fires, a shot sounds out, he drops to the floor.*

What's going on?

KORKILOFF: Nothing! We play Russian Roulette.

AUDUBON: Oh! That's all right, then. Your turn, Léon . . . May I call you Léon?

PLANTIN: With pleasure! (*He sings.*)

> March on
> March on
> March on, march on, march on
> Let's march with measured tread
> Along a road that's red
> March on
> March on.

Same business as before of refrain. ROLAND, *who has taken the revolver, twirled the cylinder and pressed the trigger, crumples to the ground as a shot goes off.* KORKILOFF *and* LAVESTE *choke with laughter.*

Hey, that game of yours looks amusing. Show me how it works. (*He takes the revolver.*)

KORKILOFF (*sings*):

> March on
> March on
> March on, march on, march on
> Let's march like Buddhist bonze
> Along a road of bronze
> March on
> March on.

He is convulsed with laughter. PLANTIN *pulls the trigger and crumples to the floor as the bullet passes through* KORKILOFF, *who also drops dead.**

AUDUBON: Fantastic! Two with a single shot! Your turn, Laveste!

During the following song, JUILLET *recovers the revolver, goes through the same business as the others, and drops dead at the end of the verse.*

LAVESTE:

> March on
> March on
> March on, march on, march on
> Let's march through thick and thin
> Along a road of bum-skin
> March on
> March on.

AUDUBON: Right on the button! (*He takes the revolver.*)

---

* In one of the two typed copies of the "final" version of the play, the author added a marginal note at this juncture, indicating a change in plot which would have had Korkiloff die by his own hand in exactly the same manner as the others, *after* the succeeding verse of the song had been sung by Laveste. But the author failed to provide the changes in the text which this additional piece of business would have necessitated. (*Translator's note.*)

Explain to me how it works, you're the only one
having any fun . . .

LAVESTE: Simple as child's play! You put a bullet in the
cylinder . . . give it a twirl . . . then pull the trigger
. . . like this . . .

A shot rings out and he falls dead.

AUDUBON: Oh, how super! Let me try! (*He loads the
weapon and twirls the cylinder.*) One . . . two . . .
three . . . (*Pulls the trigger. Nothing happens.*) Damn!
Lost! (*He twirls again, pulls the trigger, the gun fires
and a picture drops off the wall.*) Ha! Nearly! (*He
tries a third time, the gun goes off and he drops dead,
crying out:*) I've won!

*A thin, small sound suddenly swells up: it is the
"Marseillaise" being played on a reed-pipe. Enter
DUPONT, dressed in full ceremonial uniform, his saber
at the slope, drawing behind him a small cannon on
wheels. He crosses the stage singing.*

> March on
> March on
> March on, march on, march on
> Let's march with heads aloft
> Along a road that's soft
> March on
> March on.

CURTAIN